HISTORIC ILLINOIS

A Tour of the State's
Top National Landmarks

Susan O'Connor Davis

Globe
Pequot

Essex, Connecticut

For Lucy—

A life now past, yet ever present

Globe Pequot

An imprint of Globe Pequot, the trade division of
The Rowman & Littlefield Publishing Group, Inc.
4501 Forbes Blvd., Ste. 200
Lanham, MD 20706
www.rowman.com

Distributed by NATIONAL BOOK NETWORK

British Library Cataloguing in Publication Information available

Library of Congress Cataloging-in-Publication Data available
Names: Davis, Susan O'Connor, author.
Title: Historic Illinois : a tour of the state's top national landmarks /
    Susan O'Connor Davis.
Description: Essex, Connecticut : Globe Pequot, [2022] | Includes index.
Identifiers: LCCN 2022017999 (print) | LCCN 2022018000 (ebook) | ISBN
    9781493055395 (paperback) | ISBN 9781493055401 (epub)
Subjects: LCSH: Historic sites--Illinois--Guidebooks. | Historic
    buildings--Illinois--Guidebooks. | Illinois--Buildings, structures,
    etc.--Guidebooks. | Illinois--History.
Classification: LCC F542 .D38 2022 (print) | LCC F542 (ebook) | DDC
    917.73--dc23/eng/20220427
LC record available at https://lccn.loc.gov/2022017999
LC ebook record available at https://lccn.loc.gov/2022018000

CONTENTS

URBAN DEVELOPMENT, ILLINOIS 1869–1900 53

SOCIAL REFORM, ILLINOIS 1880–1925 75

TO NEW HEIGHTS, ILLINOIS 1888–1916 87

THE PRAIRIE SCHOOL ERA, ILLINOIS 1889–1909 117

THE BLACK EXPERIENCE, ILLINOIS 1905–1951 141

TOWARD THE MODERN WORLD, ILLINOIS 1900–1967 151

INTRODUCTION

Time goes, you say? Ah no!
Alas, time stays, we go.

—Austin Dobson, "The Paradox of Time"

Twenty years ago, the University of Chicago sold the last vacant parcel of land owned by the institution in the nearby historic district of South Kenwood. At that time the overgrown lot was frequented by dog lovers in the warm months, while city plows deposited mounds of heavy snow in the winter. Before long an award-winning house designed by noted architect John Vinci rose on the site.

Urban legend had it that the house that previously graced Greenwood Avenue had been torn down in error. A professor renting the house came home one afternoon to find a wrecking crew on-site, according to a neighbor. While that may seem

The Fountain of Time—Loredo Taft, sculptor. Susan O'Connor

improbable, every spring pieces of that house work their way through the warming soil. Bathroom tiles, cabinet hinges, shards of dinner plates—each find a reminder that we are not the first to make a life here.

It was not until years later, while searching for images for my first book, *Chicago's Historic Hyde Park*, and living in that Vinci creation, that I discovered a sepia-colored photograph of the earlier house. Franklin Ames's home faced west; the afternoon sun warmed the red brick façade and cast deep shadows on the classically designed porch. And there tucked away in the corner of the photograph was a square wrought iron fence post, one that marks the spot to this day.

Such is the value of discovery, linking us to the past and deepening our understanding of the present. Old photographs, treasured stories, and archival maps each demonstrate, so clearly, how the roads we walk today were not so long ago very different places.

In that vein, there are over 2,600 sites across the country designated National Historic Landmarks—recognized as places that possess exceptional value in illustrating our heritage. The program is administered by the National Park Service (NPS), and its roots can be traced to the Historic Sites Act of 1935. Under the auspices of the Secretary of the Interior, thousands of nationally significant sites across the country have been identified and evaluated, sometimes purchased and thankfully preserved.

When approached to curate a tour of those landmarks in the state of Illinois, I was curious to do so by contemplating how we have lived, and how our landscape has evolved over time. Rather than consider the sites in geographic isolation, my hope was to give a broader perspective to the reader by organizing the sites relative to the passage of time.

Thus we begin in deep southern Illinois where, a thousand years ago, Indigenous peoples built massive ceremonial mounds with surrounding population centers. We move northward along the Mississippi as the French interact with Native Americans, toward a transfer of power to the geographical center of the state, Springfield. Northward the march of progress continues, with prairies plowed and canals dug—the mighty Mississippi is connected to Eastern cities through what would become the hub of Chicago.

The heart of Chicago burned to the ground and within a decade, the notion of tall buildings that would culminate in towering skyscrapers began to gather steam. A century turned, the world soon erupted in conflict, and the power of science was unleashed. And through it all the notion of home, and all that entails, provides a linking thread.

My wish had been to hop in the car, head west to the Mississippi River, and take a hard left to see each site firsthand. Although the pandemic put an end to that dream, I did venture to sites when possible and assembled archival images of those inaccessible during a statewide lockdown. In the end this document became a study of structure, from cave dwellers to urban high-rise occupants, from those who traveled with all they owned to the gilded age when more was never enough.

I hope the result provides the reader with a rich context for a thought-provoking examination not only of architecture but also of the state's social and political history—and the divergent needs of the changing population. There were dark chapters in the process, from removal of Native Americans to slavery and its lingering effects, but in the end the sites in Illinois are noteworthy examples of what can be achieved both in architecture and in society.

Join me on this journey, as we shake off the confines of lockdown and divisiveness that gripped our attention in 2021. Let's look across the landscape and the spectrum of time—a backward and appreciative glance toward what collectively brought us to this marvelous place we now call home. For a richer understanding of our collective history not only increases an appreciation of our surroundings, but allows us to view the world from a different perspective.

The great novelist Saul Bellow once remarked he could not walk a block in Chicago without remembering who had lived here and who had died here. "You have to live with all these extinguished lives," he said, "and because you've encouraged your own sentimentality and nostalgia about a place, perhaps you feel it all the more."

There are many to thank for their guidance and assistance in this project. Distinguished architect and preservationist John Vinci once again offered his wisdom and perspective. My husband, Allison, and daughter, Jordan, provided encouragement and support as well as the love of another Ridgeback. Kevin Eatinger responded to requests for photography with a ready and able camera. James Caufield and Bill Zbaren lent images from their trove of archives. Editor Amy Lyons offered time when most needed; Chris Fischer, diligent editing and guidance. Cindy Marchessault Hurst, Lori Belknap, Brian Butler, Cynthia Waddick, Molly McKenzie, Susan Haake, and Tim Townsend kindly offered to read entries or gave advice on their specific fields of expertise. The resources of the Library of Congress were invaluable, including the 1930s images from the Historic American Buildings Survey and the magical photographs taken by Carol Highsmith.

And to all the others who shared their stories, images, and insight—my thanks.

—Susan O'Connor Davis
Chicago | November 2021

BEFORE THE
WRITTEN WORD

ILLINOIS 7000 BC–1400 AD

The past isn't dead and buried. In fact, it isn't even past.
—PRESIDENT BARACK OBAMA, 2008 (AFTER WILLIAM FAULKNER)

Mississippi River Valley farmland. Susan O'Connor

Modoc Rock Shelter. Susan O'Connor

Modoc Rock Shelter, 7,000 BC–1,000 BC
Bluff Road, Prairie du Rocher, Randolph County;
no hours, no admission charged

As mile-deep ice edged northward tens of thousands of years ago, the receding glaciers shaped the fertile terrain of Illinois. They scraped the land, moving huge amounts of earth and carving cliffs in some areas, while creating a nearly flat terrain in most others. The sediment composed of rock, clay, and sand eventually broke down to become the fertile soil that covers much of the state. As the climate warmed, new types of plants appeared while older mammals unable to adjust moved to new environments or disappeared. And ancient peoples migrated to the rich ecology of the confluence of rivers in southern Illinois.

The Modoc Rock Shelter site is an indentation at the bottom of a sandstone bluff, one that stretches for nearly eighty miles at the edge of the Mississippi River Valley. Acres of rich, flat farmland extend from the river east to the impressive cliffs, where there is an undercut section that does not look particularly inviting today. However, excavations indicate the floor level was originally much lower, and that space was large enough to provide shelter from the elements for early inhabitants of the area. Artifacts found in layer after layer of the soil indicate Archaic period Indians, including both hunting parties and longer-term occupants, used the space over the course of some six thousand years.

The Archaic Indians typically inhabited deciduous forests, living in small settlements for short periods of time before moving on to where resources were found to be more plentiful. Theirs was a subsistence economy, relying on natural resources to provide for basic needs and taking advantage of natural shelters such as at Modoc. However, they also constructed simple lodgings, as archaeologists have found evidence at other sites of structures with support posts that were possibly covered with reed mats. Animal skin tents made with sticks may have been used for temporary shelters during food gathering and hunting expeditions, all of which were transported on foot. When it came time to move on, their few belongings were carried along.

The Archaic period was a time of change for the early inhabitants of Illinois, and subsequent eras would become increasingly transformative. The Indigenous people would continue their hunting and gathering way of life, but slowly become less nomadic. Signifying the importance of this site, the Modoc Rock Shelter was designated a National Historic Landmark in 1961.

Kincaid Mounds, AD 1000–1400
New Cut Road, Brookport; kincaidmoundsorg@gmail.com;
no admission charged

In the late 1800s a white clapboard house was built atop a prehistoric mound near the Ohio River in southern Illinois. The owner, Thomas J. Kincaid, likely knew nothing of the Indigenous peoples that had periodically lived in this area since Archaic times. Those inhabitants evolved from a hunting and gathering subsistence to become more sedentary farmers centuries before Kincaid established his farm in the bottomlands of the river.

The Mississippian people came from long distances to various sites in southern Illinois about 1000 AD, where they established culturally similar yet distinct communities. Straddling Massac and Pope Counties, Kincaid Mounds is one of the larger prehistoric Native American sites in Illinois. The mounds stretch along the banks of Avery Lake, in an area known as the Black Bottom. There are competing theories for the origin of the name: the rich soil that is replenished annually by the overflow of the Ohio River, the heavy forest and swampy character of the landscape, or the Free Blacks who later settled the area.

The Mississippians who settled in the Black Bottom lived a more sedentary life than their ancestors. They were able to do so because of a stable food supply,

Kincaid Mounds. Hanna Holborn Gray Special Collections Research Center, University of Chicago Library

cultivating corn, squash and beans. The bounty of food enabled the growth of population centers and over the course of 300 years about thirty flat-topped earthen mounds were constructed.

Five or six of the largest mounds were situated around a large central plaza that was used for ceremonies. Sun-worshipping chiefs lived and ruled atop these thirty-foot-tall structures, which were created by stacking baskets of soil and clay one on top of another. Ceremonial buildings and temples were constructed on higher grounds for the ruling elite, with a protective wood stockade encircling the complex. Smaller hamlets of ten or so buildings and thatch-roofed homes were built in the surrounding bottomlands for Mississippian families.

Most of the Mississippian settlements were abandoned for reasons unknown (and likely complicated) by the early decades of the fifteenth century. After the Indigenous peoples left the area, there were groups who traversed through deep southern Illinois, either along the river or hunting in the hills. However, there is no evidence of a residential presence until the French erected Fort Massac in 1757, which drew in small contingents of Native Americans for trading purposes.

Cahokia Mounds, AD 1050–1350
30 Ramey Street, Collinsville; (618) 346-5160; cahokiamounds.org; entrance is free of charge, a donation is suggested

The remains of the most sophisticated native civilization north of Mexico are preserved at Cahokia Mounds State Historic Site. Collinsville Road cuts through the heart of the 2,200-acre tract, bisecting the archeological remnants of what was once one of the great cities of the world. As at the Kincaid site, Mississippian residents were accomplished builders—erecting a variety of structures, from practical homes to monumental public works. Their technological accomplishments included the construction of massive earthen mounds that served as elevated platforms for structures related to public officials, and surrounding wooden stockades.

Today it is hard to grasp the size and complexity of Cahokia; there were at one time more than a hundred packed earth mounds at Cahokia, arranged around four vast open plazas aligned on the cardinal directions. At the center was a tiered pyramid rising one hundred feet, its orientation tied to sunrise on the summer solstice. Height here was symbolic of power; these imposing structures rose above an otherwise flat landscape and demonstrated the strength and success of this Mississippian society. Personal, political, religious, and social attitudes each found expression in the earthen architecture—reflective of a common vision and deeper meaning in their lives.

Cahokia as it may have appeared c.1150 by Michael Hampshire. Courtesy of Cahokia Mounds State Historic Site

Mist in the Grand Plaza. Courtesy Daniel Seurer (danseurer.com) and the Cahokia Mounds State Historic Site

At its pinnacle Cahokia had a population of over ten thousand with many more living in the outlying towns and farms, stretching fifty miles in every direction. With thousands of pole and thatch houses and a society ruled by powerful chiefs, this cultural center was a great force along the Mississippi River. Rhythms were dominated by the seasons; when spring came residents set out to plant the fields, and at harvest time everyone helped to gather the crops. House building, mound construction, and other public works filled the balance of the year. Although it was probably a male-dominated society, some women would have leadership roles, while those of lower status spent much of their day in food preparation, were skilled potters, and made fine baskets, mats, and fabrics from the inner bark of local cedar trees.

Why did the Mississippians leave this remarkable assemblage of mounds, plazas, houses, and palisades? There are few signs of human habitation here from 1400 to about 1650, when the Illini Indians arrived in the area. Scholars offer varying suggestions: There was a cooling of temperatures around 1250, an overreliance on corn as a staple of diet may have led to malnutrition, while living in a high-density area may have fostered poor sanitation and disease. In the end, we do not have a definitive answer—but through the sites at Modoc, Kincaid, and Cahokia, we witness early Native American society as highly adaptive and creative.

FRENCH INDIAN INFLUENCES

ILLINOIS 1500–1800

I have not sold my lands. I will not sell them.
I have not signed any treaty, and will not sign any.
I am not going to leave my lands.
—MENOMINEE (POTAWATOMI), 1838

The Chicago Portage National Historic Site marks the western end of the historic portage linking the Great Lakes to the Mississippi River. French explorers Father Marquette and Louis Jolliet came into the vicinity in the 1670s. The sculpture at the site, by Guido Rebechini, depicts them with native guides and was dedicated in May 1930. Susan O'Connor

Starved Rock, 1500–1800
2668 East 75th Road, Oglesby; (815) 667-4726;
starvedrock.org; no admission charged

The bluff known today as Starved Rock was formed by rushing waters as glaciers receded across the state at the end of the Ice Age over thirteen thousand years ago. As temperatures warmed, Indigenous Hopewellian, Woodland, and Mississippian cultures came to this area as early as 8000 BC. The most recent group of Native Americans to inhabit the locale along the Illinois river were the Peoria, an Algonquin-speaking tribe of the Illinois Confederacy, who thrived between 1500 and the early 1700s.

In 1673, French explorers Louis Jolliet and Father Jacques Marquette passed through this territory on their return from a pioneering voyage down the Mississippi. When Marquette came back two years later, he founded the Mission of the Immaculate Conception, the first Christian mission in the state, at Old Kaskaskia Village across the river and to the east of Starved Rock. Also known as the Grand Village of the Illinois, 7-8,000 inhabitants lived here, sheltered in long arbor-like dwellings covered with reed mats. The enclave was brutally destroyed by rival Iroquois Indians in 1680 and the site abandoned. Old Kaskaskia Village is a National Historic Landmark, but the land is privately held with no access permitted.

Soon the French claimed this region (and the whole of the Mississippi Valley) and in the winter of 1682–83 built Fort St. Louis on the outcropping known today as Starved Rock. For nine years the location offered a strategic position on the Illinois River and was a key part of a large French-Indian alliance until the fort was abandoned in 1691.

During this time the Native American population grew to nearly fifteen thousand inhabitants living in the vicinity of the fort and trading post. Indians of the Illinois Confederacy lived a cyclical seasonal existence. Every spring, members would gather at their village and plant crops nearby. Summer months meant hunting buffalo and a return to the village for the harvest. Corn was dried in early fall, and then the Peoria dispersed to small winter encampments, hunting and procuring hides to trade until the spring, when the cycle began again.

Legend has it Starved Rock was named for an event that occurred near the Peoria village along the Illinois River before the arrival of Marquette and Jolliet. After Pontiac (a rival Ottawa chief) was slain at a tribal council in the spring of 1769, retribution followed. During one of the clashes that occurred to avenge his killing, the Peoria fled downriver from their village to a 125-foot sandstone summit for protection. Tribes of Potawatomi and Ottawa surrounded the rock, remaining there until the Peoria starved to death—thus giving the rock its name.

There are inconsistencies to the story, with some claiming the Peoria were killed at the base of the rock following a tremendous battle. However, excavations at the

French Canyon. Kevin Eatinger

site found no evidence of a large massacre. As well, British accounts of the time have no references to a large confrontation and refer to a thriving tribe of Illinois in multiple accounts in years after the event.

Starved Rock was known by many names—Le Rocher to the French, the Rock to the British, and Little Rocks or Small Rocks to others. Not until 1834 does the name Starved Rock appear; was the event an actual historical occurrence or just an age-old tale?

Many researchers believe the legend is based on an actual event that did occur at the rock, but in the year 1722. An aging Fox chief was determined to take revenge for the death of his nephew who was burned to death by the Peoria. Ouashala told the French, "I had resolved on setting out, to destroy their village [the Peoria village at Starved Rock] . . . and spare no lives whatever." French records confirm this battle and a truce that was then negotiated between the tribes.

Two centuries later the Civilian Conservation Corps began construction on Starved Rock Lodge. The highlight of the charming 1930s building is a massive limestone fireplace, centered within the structure of unhewn logs, clapboard, and wood shingles. Today Starved Rock State Park offers visitors thirteen miles of hiking trails that meander through canyons and past scenic, seasonal waterfalls.

Fort de Chartres, 1720–1772
1350 State Route 155, Prairie du Rocher; (618) 284-7230;
fortdechartres.us; grounds are open; a donation is suggested

When French explorers came to Illinois nearly 350 years ago, the landscape looked quite different than it appears today. Bison and elk roamed prairies filled with blue-stem, switchgrass, coneflower, and blazing star that stretched for hundreds of miles. Bear and mountain lions prowled a patchwork of forests and marshes. And the southern Illinois floodplain known as the American Bottom became a favored location of fur traders and French settlers.

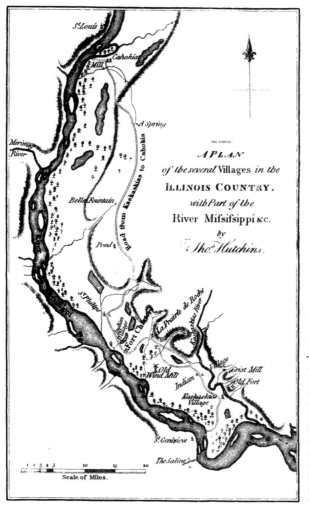

Thomas Hutchins's 1778 map of the fertile floodplain known as the American Bottoms. Map of the Several Villages in the Illinois Country with Part of the River Mississippi &c. (facsimile) by Thomas Hutchins. *The Conspiracy of Pontiac and the Indian War after the Conquest of Canada,* Vol. I, by Francis Parkman, 1851. 6th ed., 1870. Project Gutenberg, 2012.

The north wall of Fort de Chartres. Susan O'Connor

Located on the east bank of the Mississippi River, between the river and the nearby cliffs, Fort de Chartres served as the seat of French government in the territory then known as Upper Louisiana. The earliest stockade fort on this site was erected in 1720 and two subsequent structures were also built of hewed timbers and planks. The massive stone fort seen today is a partial reconstruction of a fourth structure that was completed in 1753. Built of stone quarried from the bluffs of nearby Prairie du Rocher, this impressive fortification was key to France's military presence in the area.

After the French and Indian War (also known as the Seven Years' War) ended in 1763, France ceded much of its territory in North America, including what is now Illinois, to Great Britain. The royal flag of Louis XV was replaced by the red cross of St. George, marking a new era. British troops occupied the fort for a brief period, renaming the structure Fort Cavendish. The 1783 Treaty of Paris was signed by Britain and the colonies, thus ending the American Revolution.

As the country expanded westward, the abandoned fort slowly deteriorated; the south wall collapsed into the Mississippi, locals scavenged the stone for other purposes, and trees and vines began to cover the remains of the walls. In 1913 the site was acquired by the State of Illinois and underwent many years of restoration. The thick eighteen-foot-high north wall has been rebuilt, complete with bastions at each corner and an imposing gatehouse. The fort's interior includes the powder magazine, Guard's House, and King's Storehouse—now home to the fort's museum.

Church of the Holy Family, 1799
116 Church Street, Cahokia; (618) 337-4548; holyfamily1699.org; grounds are open and tours of the interior are by appointment

Located in a town named for an Illinois tribe, Holy Family Church is the oldest continuous Catholic parish in the United States. Founded by Canadian missionaries with a purpose of converting the Native Americans to Christianity, the site not far from the Mississippi River marks the first permanent settlement in the Illinois country. The original church was christened on May 14, 1699 and stood here until destroyed by fire in 1740.

The eye-catching log church structure visitors see today was built in 1799 in a similar style to the one erected a century earlier. By this time Cahokia had grown to be a center of influence in the upper Mississippi Valley. It was a bustling French colonial town, with three thousand inhabitants and a thriving business district that included twenty-four brothels. Hence perhaps, the need to rebuild the church.

Constructed of black walnut timbers in traditional French Colonial post-on-sill construction, the log church is only one of five built in this style that still exist in North America. It is a largely unaltered example of what was once a common construction form.

Timber framing of the period involved setting large vertical log posts into sills that in turn rested on some type of level footing. Here the heavy timbers measure 12 by 6 inches, are 14 feet high and placed one foot apart. The spaces between the timbers are filled with a mixture of small stones and clay, known as pierrotage. The walls of this church slope inward about eight inches, and a single beam runs the length of the church to support the roof. No nails were used in this or the original church; wooden pegs secured this visually striking structure.

Church of the Holy Family. Susan O'Connor

Buried in the adjacent cemetery are members of an important early family of Cahokia, the Jarrots. One of a handful of gravestones that have survived is that of Julie Beauvais Jarrot (1780–1875). But also buried here are hundreds of other baptized Blacks, whites, and Native Americans in graves no longer marked. Jarrot's slave Joseph is said to be interred on the same grounds (although records do not confirm that) and each played a role in the elimination of slavery in the state.

Joseph was born into slavery; his grandmother had been purchased by a French settler. In the 1840s he sued his owner, the widow Julie Jarrot, for

Gravestone of Julie Beauvais Jarrot.
Susan O'Connor

back wages in the amount of five dollars for the previous five years of work. In effect, he was suing for his freedom. When the local court found for Julie, Joseph appealed.

In 1845 the Illinois Supreme Court overturned the judgment, clarifying that the 1787 Northwest Ordinance prohibited slavery and servitude in the state.

Pierre Menard Residence, 1802
4230 Kaskaskia Road, Ellis Grove; (618) 284-7230: grounds are open; a donation is suggested

Pierre Menard (1766–1844) was a prosperous merchant and well-regarded citizen of Kaskaskia in the early 1800s. His Southern French Colonial–style house was erected on the gentle slope of a bluff overlooking the wide Mississippi River. Built of hand-hewn timbers pegged together beneath a low-hipped roof, the house was constructed in a style reflective of his standing in the community.

Born in Montreal, an ambitious young Menard left home at the age of fifteen to find adventure on an expedition. Traveling to the Northwest Territory in 1790, he settled in this center of commerce—bartering with Native Americans, supplying provisions to fur-traders and selling goods to residents.

Menard's first wife died in 1804, leaving him a widower with four children. Two years later he married dark-haired Angelique Saucier, seventeen years his junior. They had eight more children, conceived at a time when a large family was considered an economic advantage.

Pierre Menard Residence. Susan O'Connor

Kitchen, Pierre Menard House. Historic American Buildings Survey, Creator, and Joseph Champaigne. 1933. Library of Congress

When Congress organized the Illinois Territory in the winter of 1809, carving out a portion of the Northwest Territory with Kaskaskia as the capital, Menard became president of the council. Illinois became a state in 1818, and Menard achieved his most noteworthy achievement, as the state's first lieutenant governor.

Menard's holdings encompassed over one thousand acres with a pecan orchard of fifteen hundred trees and several outbuildings, including quarters for enslaved people. The home state of Abraham Lincoln is not typically thought of as associated with slavery, but it was part of everyday life for over a century. The story of servitude began in 1719; a French businessman brought five hundred enslaved people to work on a mine at nearby Fort de Chartres. When the venture failed, he sold them to nearby residents. In 1787 the Northwest Ordinance outlawed slavery—but only prohibited *newly enslaved people*. Existing ones would remain in servitude, held as chattel, taxed as personal property, and sold at will.

Menard was one of the largest holders of enslaved people in the area, and his reliance on their labor was an integral part of his success. He owned twenty-two slaves, working as farm laborers in his beloved orchard, while others were domestic servants in this distinctive house. The enslaved people resided in quarters behind the residence, while the Menards lived on the main level of a home that depended on their service. Every conceivable domestic role was undertaken by enslaved people—they prepared the food in the stone kitchen behind the house and were also the nannies, nurses, laundresses, and cleaners for the family.

Menard left public office in 1822, as economic forces were drawing importance away from the towns along the Mississippi River. Kaskaskia had been considered a place of culture and refinement, but as wealth and population shifted northward in the new state, the capital was moved from Kaskaskia to Vandalia. Menard remained a respected figure in his elegant home on the bluff until his death in 1844. There is no evidence this affluent gentleman emancipated any enslaved people during his lifetime.

Nicholas V. Jarrot Residence, 1807–1810
124 East First Street, Cahokia; (618) 332-1782; jarrotmansion.org; grounds are open, and tours of the interior are by appointment only

As the nineteenth century dawned the village of Cahokia was a thriving town in the Northwest Territory, an area established by the newly formed American republic. The venerable Jarrot residence is perhaps the oldest brick house in the Mississippi Valley; construction began in 1807. In a clear departure from vertical timber structures, the red brick Federal-style house demonstrates the introduction of new construction types and materials to the developing frontier.

Jarrot Residence. Susan O'Connor

Central Hall, Jarrot Residence. Susan O'Connor

Nicholas Vital Jarrot (1764–1820) became one of the leading citizens of the Illinois territory, which was organized in the winter of 1809. He had arrived in America without many resources, traveled from Baltimore to New Orleans, ventured up the Mississippi River, and settled at Cahokia. Beginning in the fur trade, Jarrot then opened a small general store, expanded into the operation of several small mills, and started a ferry service that crossed the Mississippi. However, it was the acquisition of real estate that brought him a great fortune. By 1815 he had amassed upward of twenty-five thousand acres of land and his wealth and status were well known.

After his first wife died in childbirth, Jarrot married an aristocratic young French woman named Julie Ste. Gemme de Beauvais. For several years they lived in a small wooden house across the street from Holy Family Church. But the ambitious Jarrot desired a house that reflected his increasing status, and it would take several years to complete the structure to his satisfaction.

The two-story house was constructed of hand-pressed brick fired in a kiln on-site. The home was solidly built, with eighteen-inch-thick walls resting on a substantial stone foundation and black walnut timbers. And it was stylishly fashioned; expensive wallpapers and vivid paint colors graced the home. There were five rooms on the main level, each warmed by a fireplace, with several more on the second level adjacent to a large pine-planked ballroom.

Jarrot, in his roles as lawyer, judge, and captain of the militia, was quite social. The couple held numerous receptions, parties, and balls, each described as polished and elegant affairs. In particular, the ballroom was said to be the scene of much gaiety. Guests were received before a large fireplace on the main level; after dinner was served the party moved to the ballroom for card games and dancing.

In its two hundred years, the house has had only five owners and remains remarkably intact. Yet the home also bears the mark of a tumultuous event in Illinois history. At 2:15 in the morning of December 16, 1811, residents of the frontier town were jolted from their beds by a violent earthquake. Extending outward from the epicenter at New Madrid 175 miles to the south, the ground heaved and pitched, damaging every building in Cahokia save for the church. As people were starting to rebuild that winter, there were two more major earthquakes, each of a magnitude of 7.5 or greater. The severity of these events toppled the east chimney, but the Jarrot House endured.

Nicholas Vital Jarrot became ill while tending one of his mills and died at the age of fifty-six. He is buried in the cemetery next to the Church of the Holy Family, just a short walk from their home. The village of Cahokia declined rapidly with the rise of St. Louis, but the widow Jarrot remained in her mansion for many years. She died in East St. Louis in 1875 at the ripe old age of ninety-five and is buried next to her husband.

BEGINNING ANEW

ILLINOIS 1784–1880

The portage's single hotel was a barracks, its streets were pig-wallows, and all the long summer night the Pottawattomies mourned beside that river: down in the barracks the horse-dealers and horse-stealers were making a night of it again. Whiskey-and-vermilion hustlers, painting the night vermilion.

In the Indian grass the Indians listened: they too had lived by night.

—NELSON ALGREN, FOLKLORE OF THE MIDDLE GROUND, 1951

Chicago in 1820. Print showing Native Americans engaged in fur trading on the banks of a river or lake at the settlement of Chicago; Chicago Lithographing Co., c. 1867. Library of Congress Prints and Photographs Division

Jean Baptiste Point du Sable Homesite, c.1784–1800
Michigan Avenue, just north of the Chicago River;
no admission, no hours

When Jean La Lime purchased the farm and cabin of Jean Baptiste Point du Sable (c.1745–1818) in 1800 it was a lonely outpost on the north side of a sluggish river lined with cattails. The locale known as Checkagou—presumably named for an abundant and potent wild leek—was inhabited by Native Americans. Much of the area was a web of marshy wetlands and dry ridges, with wooded groves that interrupted otherwise damp and rough terrain. To the east was a vast lake, and to the west tallgrass prairies stretched as far as one could see.

Over the years local Potawatomie established economic and kinship ties with French-Canadian fur traders. Into this milieu came a Black trader named Jean Baptiste Point du Sable. He traveled around the southern end of the lake after leaving his position as a manager for the British in eastern Michigan, arriving in Chicago about 1784. Du Sable married a Potawatomie woman named Kitihawa, and they had a son Jean and daughter Susanne.

There is little evidence of du Sable's life prior to 1770, but there are plenty of stories about his African origins. Some place his birth in Haiti; others present him as the son of a pirate ship's mate and a freed enslaved person called Suzanne. Regardless of his birthplace, Jean Baptiste Point du Sable is the earliest recorded resident of the settlement that grew to become the mighty city of Chicago.

Described as a large, handsome man and wealthy trader by a 1794 visitor, the bill of sale for du Sable's property confirms at least one of those adjectives. In exchange for twelve hundred dollars, the buyer received two barns, a horse-drawn mill, a bakehouse, a poultry house, and a smokehouse, in addition to the twenty-two by forty-foot log cabin. The sale of that rather rough structure included an array of fine furniture and paintings.

Du Sable left Chicago for St. Charles, Missouri, in 1800, where he operated a ferry across the Missouri River. He died in 1818 and was buried in an unmarked grave. The burial register of St. Charles Borromeo cemetery simply describes du Sable as "negre."

Sculptor Eric Blome's bronze bust of the first nonindigenous settler in Chicago denotes du Sable's homestead site today, on the east side of Michigan Avenue just north of the Chicago River.

Bronze of Jean Baptiste Point du Sable with bas-relief sculpture on the Michigan Avenue bridge house. Susan O'Connor

New Philadelphia Townsite, 1836–1880
Broad Street and Pike County Highway 2, Barry;
newphiladelphiail.org; no admission, no hours

Although this parcel of land about four miles outside of the town of Barry is vacant, it has quite a story to tell. Here lived a man born into slavery, a man who purchased freedom for his family, helped to secure property rights for people of color in Illinois, fostered an integrated community, and gave his descendants a proud name. And all that took place before the Civil War.

"Free Frank" McWorter (1777–1854) was enslaved for forty-two years. Born in South Carolina, he was taken to his owner's new farmstead in the Kentucky wilderness, where by 1810 he began hiring out his own time. Enslavers like George McWhorter, Frank's master, earned additional capital by allowing enslaved people to work on other enterprises. Any money earned above what was owed to their enslavers could be kept.

The funds from his work mining and processing saltpeter enabled Frank to purchase property, but most importantly, the ability to negotiate freedom for his family. Through his efforts, his wife Lucy was freed in 1817, and he was able to secure his own freedom two years later. Free Frank then either sold or traded his acreage in the slave state of Kentucky; on September 30, 1830, he became a landowner and was bound for a new life in west central Illinois.

But remaining a free person was tricky business for a Black man or woman. As they undertook the five hundred–mile journey to the fertile lands of Pike County, Frank, Lucy, and four of their children faced not only the typical hazards of travel—bad roads, deep winter snows, and robbery—they also had to guard against slave catchers who could destroy their papers and sell them to the cotton, rice, or sugar plantations of the Deep South.

Armed with his papers and the required Certificate of Character, fifty-three-year-old Frank and his ox-pulled covered wagon finally arrived at their property in the spring of 1831. He proceeded to build a log house near a stand of woods, while the remaining prairie lands were used for farming. Frank's illiteracy did not hinder his endeavors; he continued to purchase land in Pike County's Hadley Township and in 1835 acquired an eighty-acre tract just south of his farm for the sum of one hundred dollars, with hopes of founding a town.

That same year, Free Frank petitioned the Illinois General Assembly to take a surname; this was a crucial step, as it solidified the legality of Frank's holdings. A version of the name of his former master McWhorter was requested. In 1836, the newly named Frank McWorter officially registered his town of 144 lots. Surveyors platted the town of New Philadelphia, where 60 by 120-foot parcels were arranged in a typical grid pattern along the two main avenues, Main Street and Broad Way.

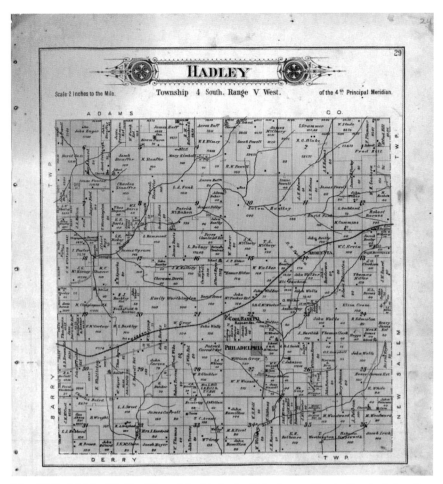

New Philadelphia, Hadley Township. Plat book of Pike County, Illinois. Geo. A. Ogle & Co, F. Bourquin, and Balliet & Volk, 1895. Library of Congress

There was no question as to McWorter's purpose—the sale of the lots would be used to purchase the remaining members of his family from slavery.

At the time there were no nearby towns, yet Frank continued to acquire land, eventually amassing eight hundred acres by 1839. The development moved slowly, for by 1847 only three log houses had been built on Frank's lots. But the enclave began to grow in the period before the Civil War. By 1850 New Philadelphia had the makings of a flourishing town, with two shoemakers, two postmasters, a merchant, a cabinetmaker, a blacksmith, a wheelwright, and a Baptist minister listed as residents.

New Philadelphia attracted both Black and white residents and with its location just fifty miles from the slaveholding state of Missouri, was a known station on the Underground Railroad. The town was at its most prosperous in 1854, the year Free Frank passed away. By the time of his death at the age of seventy-seven, Frank McWorter had purchased the freedom of sixteen individuals.

Following the Civil War, the population of his town decreased from its peak of 160; New Philadelphia lost its town status in the 1880s and reverted to farmland over subsequent decades. The former town is now an open field, and a lone highway marker identifies the site amid cornfields, trees and gentle hills stretching far as the eye can see.

Dr. John Kennicott Residence, 1836-1856
1421 Milwaukee Avenue, Glenview; (847) 299-6096;
glenviewparks.org/thegrove; no admission charged,
trails open dawn to dusk

North suburban Glenview was very much a part of the Illinois frontier in 1836, the year Dr. John A. Kennicott arrived from New Orleans with his family. Kennicott was one of the first physicians in an area then called West Northfield. He claimed several hundred acres of land on the ridge of a prairie east of the Des Plaines River, which were christened "The Grove." There were only ten families in the area when the doctor and his wife Mary erected the log cabin where the family lived for twenty years, until the Gothic Revival house currently on the site was constructed.

Although much of his time was spent in his medical practice, John Kennicott's interest in horticulture grew year by year. He opened a nursery and garden on forty-five acres of the property, offering apple trees for twelve and a half cents each, plum trees for fifty cents, and a wide variety of roses, perennials, and bulbs. Kennicott's reputation as a knowledgeable nurseryman spread quickly, and he was known as a passionate promoter of progressive agricultural and horticultural practices. He became an editor at the *Prairie Farmer*, supported the first Illinois State Fair (1853), and helped create a national system of agricultural colleges.

Kennicott frequently wrote and spoke of the practical benefits of plant culture. Shade trees near a house offered welcome relief from the blazing heat of a summer day. Carefully planted evergreens, he argued, could enliven bleak winter landscapes. Understanding the addition of fruits and vegetables to one's diet could improve health, so the doctor advised *Prairie Farmer* readers to consider the nutritional benefits of fruit trees or a seasonal vegetable garden. Kennicott pointed out that carefully tended flower beds or well-placed shrubs and trees enhanced the landscape, making the family home even more pleasant.

Across the country this theme was amplified as landscape gardeners encouraged home gardening and the beautification of both rural and urban landscapes. Books published by landscape designer Andrew Jackson Downing provided the country's

Kennicott Residence. Susan O'Connor

growing population with visions of ideal home settings. These early books often featured the work of architect Alexander Jackson Davis and had an enormous effect on American taste. Carpenters used these inexpensive guides to construct wood-frame houses, set harmoniously on the landscape. Houses often featured Gothic details such as the elongated windows and the vertical board and batten siding used at the Kennicott House.

Robert Kennicott (1835-1866) was but one year old when his parents came to the Grove. Although sickly as a child, Robert flourished, exploring the plants and animals of the Grove, which came to be the passion of his life. Father and son each studied the prairies; they observed, collected, and preserved specimens while chronicling their natural surroundings in early scientific journals.

On his second expedition to Alaska, Robert met an untimely death at age thirty. An exhibition at the Grove noted Robert's contributions to science went well beyond his years. His exploration of the Northwest wilderness contributed to the 1867 decision for the United States to purchase territory (now Alaska) from Russia. And his name can be found on a glacier, rivers, and towns, in addition to several animal species.

Well over a century later, it appeared that a high-density residential development was slated to be built on Kennicott's Grove. In 1973 the Save the Grove Committee was formed, and according to the Glenview Park District, this organization played a vital role in preserving this important historic site. The picturesque 1856 Gothic Revival–style house has been carefully restored and 135 of Kennicott's original 868 acres are open to the public. The Grove also offers hiking trails, an interpretive center, a Native American longhouse, a log cabin, and the Kennicott family graveyard.

Nauvoo Historic District, 1839–1846
Hancock County; the visitor center is located at 290 North Main Street; (217) 577-2603; nauvoohistoricsites.org

In the spring of 1830, Joseph Smith founded the Church of Jesus Christ of Latter-Day Saints. Smith claimed he had been visited by Moroni, an angel who spoke to him of an ancient Hebrew text that had been lost for centuries. This holy text, which was said to have been engraved on gold plates and told the story of Israelites who lived in America in ancient times, was transcribed as the Book of Mormon.

The religion quickly gained converts, as Smith moved westward to set up communities in Ohio in 1831 and Missouri in 1838. Unaccepted for their beliefs and threatened with mob violence and bloodshed, the Latter-Day Saints fled Missouri and crossed into Illinois during the harsh winter of 1838–39. Over the course of the next few years, some sixteen thousand Latter-Day Saints settled in the area along the eastern banks of the Mississippi.

Theirs was a swampy, mosquito-infested terrain, first known as Quashquema for a Native American chief of the Sauk who occupied the area. As the Latter-Day Saints began draining the swampland, they christened the settlement Nauvoo, a Hebrew word meaning "beautiful." The city became one of the largest in Illinois at the time and was an important commercial center on the river.

By 1844 the city teemed with activity. Construction was the major industry as blacksmiths, gun shops, lumberyards, brickmakers, pottery makers, bakeries, newspapers, and schools were built. In addition to massive housing demands (three hundred homes were constructed) Nauvoo also had two large public projects underway: a four-story hotel at the river's edge and a large temple towering over the entire community.

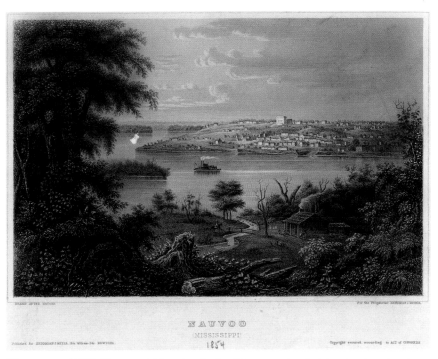

Nauvoo, ca. 1855. Hermann J. Meyer hand-colored line engraving. Smithsonian American Art Museum, Gift of International Business Machines Corporation, 1966.

The Temple of the Church of Jesus Christ of Latter-Day Saints was the center-piece of the Mormon settlement, set in a commanding position on the landscape. The majestic cupola-topped limestone structure was built on a high bluff facing westward, but life was not all bliss below. In the spring of 1844, some of Joseph Smith's most trusted followers broke from him. Within days violence ensued and Smith, as mayor of Nauvoo, declared martial law within the city. However charges were brought against him, and Smith was ordered to nearby Carthage. Awaiting trial, he and his brother Hyram were both killed.

After the death of Joseph Smith, Hancock County was gripped with fear of retaliation. Under the leadership of Brigham Young, the Mormons agreed to aban-don Nauvoo and leave the state the coming year. A continual procession of wagons began in the spring and continued through the summer of 1846, crossing westward over the Mississippi River. At the time of the exodus, Nauvoo was equal in size to Chicago; afterward its population was less than two thousand.

The massive temple was never used. Dedicated on May 1, 1846, it was stripped of everything that could be moved the following day. For two years the edifice tow-ered over a nearly deserted Nauvoo, until the evening of October 8, 1848, when it

Steeple Building, Main & Bishop Hill Streets. Susan O'Connor

the Atlantic, they journeyed westward from New York on a slow passage through the Erie Canal, followed by an eleven-day wagon trek to Chicago. From there they made their way to Bishop Hill, on foot it is told, nearly 160 miles over unbroken prairie.

The site in Henry County had been selected by Olaf Olson, a scout sent by Janson a year before their arrival. Their first autumn, twelve crude structures of earth and timber were erected, nested into a long ravine as protection from the oncoming winter. Each of the shelters offered a fireplace and bunks for thirty but little else. Winter was hard, food scarce and sanitation poor—nearly a quarter of the Jansonites died before spring came.

Yet the colony grew and prospered, as many more immigrants came from Sweden to join the utopian experiment. The colonists farmed nearly fifteen thousand acres of virgin soil and laid out a town around a central park. A church was erected, several four-story dwellings (now demolished), and sorely needed brick and frame houses. Additionally, there was a school, flax, grist and flour mills, bakery and brewery, carpenter and paint shop, and a blacksmith shop—belonging to all.

Cholera brought death to 143 members in 1849; Janson would not permit colonists to see a doctor, believing a lack of faith led to sickness. The next year another traumatic event unfolded: Janson's own death at the age of forty-one. A disgruntled colonist had a long, bitter feud with Janson, and shot him once through the heart.

The commune survived these events, argued over celibacy and the education of children, and eventually dissolved in 1861.

Today several historically significant buildings have survived to indicate life in the colony, four of which are owned by the state and managed as part of the Bishop Hill State Historic Site. The gambrel-roofed Colony Church c.1848 contains a sanctuary large enough to seat one thousand worshippers. Handsome pews of black walnut rest on a rough-hewn pine floor, lit by delicate candle chandeliers of wood and wrought iron. In a demonstration of much needed housing, the Swedes put one-room family apartments beneath the sanctuary.

The three-story cupola-topped Steeple Building dates from 1854 when it was constructed to accommodate the growing number of visitors. For reasons unknown, it was never used for that purpose and became a schoolhouse for the colony's children where the curriculum sought to keep children from straying from the faith. The stucco exterior features a Palladian-style portico topped by an octagonal tower with steeple clock.

Janson died at the height of his power; 1,000 Swedes had abandoned their homes to join him on the frontier. The colony was in a dire financial situation at the end, while the railroad and canal brought outside habits and ideas to the settlement. Today, 122 people reside in Bishop Hill. Despite its short tenure, the colony is considered a significant factor in the immigration of Swedes to America.

Colony Church. Susan O'Connor

John Deere Residence and Shop, 1837
8334 South Clinton Street, Dixon; (815) 652-4551;
visitjohndeere.com; no admission charged

The name John Deere is synonymous with the development of farm machinery. The company's namesake created the first commercially successful steel plow, and his business grew into a corporation in the ranks of the country's Fortune 500. Today Deere & Company is one of the world's largest manufacturers of agricultural machinery—and its beginnings were in the humble blacksmith shop on this site.

John Deere (1804–1886) left his native Vermont in the fall of 1836. His blacksmith business had been difficult there and he ventured westward to Grand Detour, a small, picturesque village on a horseshoe bend of the Rock River. Deere continued in his trade; however, the cast-iron plows he made on the East Coast did not work well in the heavier soil of the Illinois prairie. Deere then fashioned a blade of polished steel to shred the stubborn turf. It was a success and his enterprise quickly grew—building ten plows for local farmers in 1839, seventy-five in 1841, and one hundred the following year.

The components of the historic site include two acres of prairie restoration, a replica of the blacksmith shop, and John and Demarius Deere's home. The original portion of the house was built by Deere himself and consisted of only one room initially, where the family dined and slept. Over time the clapboard structure was enlarged to two levels with four rooms on the main level and two rooms upstairs.

The Deere family left this house when the company relocated to a site in Moline, Illinois, on the east bank of the Mississippi River.

Illinois & Michigan Canal, 1836–1848
Lockport Visitor Center, 200 W. 8th Street, Lockport; there are
several visitor centers along the length of the canal; (815) 220-1848;
iandmcanal.org

The year 1848 marks a pivotal moment in the development of the city of Chicago. When the Illinois & Michigan (I & M) Canal was completed that year, the waterway joined the Chicago River with the Illinois River at LaSalle, some ninety-six miles to the west. The canal provided a direct water link between the Great Lakes and the Mississippi River, which resulted in a shift of the center of Midwestern trade from St. Louis to Chicago, while opening a passageway to the American West.

The dream of a connecting link that would open trade and travel had its beginnings as early as the time of French explorer Louis Jolliet. He envisioned a canal cutting through prairie and swamp that would enable travel to the Gulf of Mexico with ease of navigation. This dream persisted; President James Madison referred to a

Illinois & Michigan Canal, Lift Lock No. 6, East side of DuPage River. Historic American Engineering Record, Creator, and William Gooding. Will County, Channahon, Illinois, 1968. Library of Congress

proposed route of a canal in his 1804 inaugural address. Initial surveys for the canal's route took place in 1816 but funds were not yet available, and the needed treaties were not yet in place.

The 1833 Treaty of Chicago brought an estimated three thousand Native Americans, traders, government officials, army troops, and land speculators to the then-small village to witness the dramatic proceedings as the Potawatomi ceded the last of their Illinois and Wisconsin lands. By 1836 the federal government auctioned land in Chicago and along the canal route to finance the project, and construction began.

Thousands of Irish workers were recruited to dig the I & M Canal, excavating by hand. They were housed in shantytowns and hastily built camps where sanitation was abysmal, leading to outbreaks of cholera and malaria. Working conditions were equally bad, with laborers paid a single dollar and a bit of whiskey for their back-breaking fifteen-hour days.

A series of financial problems delayed the project but in 1848 the canal was finally complete. In April the first boat traveled from New Orleans through the American heartland to Buffalo, New York, via the waterway, and soon after the Illinois landscape was transformed. Prairies and wetlands were replaced with agriculture and industry; cities and towns along the canal prospered as shipping points for the region's resources.

The investment in the canal established Chicago as the nation's largest inland port and helped transform the city into the country's fastest-growing metropolis. Chicago boomed both in terms of population and exports; shipments of corn increased eightfold, and lumber doubled. Coal and grain from the canal region, and sugar molasses and coffee from the South, passed through the city on their way to Eastern markets.

By 1864, 288 mule-drawn boats worked the canal, transporting commodities at just three miles per hour. A shift to steam-propelled boats made traffic more efficient, reaching a peak tonnage of over a million tons in 1882. Although tolls and land sales made it possible for the canal to pay off its debt in 1871, maintenance was an issue and navigating the six-foot-deep canal became increasingly difficult.

By the late 1890s commercial traffic lessened, as Chicago became the nation's railway hub, and by the late 1910s, it was virtually non-existent. The I & M Canal had outlived its usefulness and closed in 1933. Two years later the Civilian Conservation Corps restored several of the fifteen locks and started other projects intended for recreational purposes. In 1984 President Ronald Reagan signed legislation creating the Illinois & Michigan Canal National Heritage Corridor. It was hoped the resulting trails and nature preserves along the canal route would shore up the economic development of adjacent towns by emphasizing their history, while encouraging historic preservation.

LAND OF LINCOLN

ILLINOIS 1839–1876

A house divided against itself cannot stand. I believe this government cannot endure, permanently half slave and half free. I do not expect the Union to be dissolved—I do not expect the house to fall—but I do expect it will cease to be divided. It will become all one thing or all the other.
—ABRAHAM LINCOLN, ILLINOIS REPUBLICAN STATE CONVENTION,
SPRINGFIELD, JUNE 16, 1858

With the 1888 Illinois State capitol building as a backdrop, a ten-foot, six-inch bronze statue of Abraham Lincoln was dedicated on October 5, 1918, the centennial of the first meeting of the Illinois General Assembly. At the ceremony Illinois poet Vachel Lindsay recited his poem, "When Lincoln Walks at Midnight in Springfield." Engraved with Lincoln's "Farewell to Springfield" speech, the statue was the work of sculptor Andrew O'Connor. Kevin Eatinger

Old State Capitol, 1839
South Sixth & East Adams Street, Springfield; (217) 785-7960; www2.illinois.gov/dnrhistoric/Experience/Sites; a donation is suggested

When Springfield became Illinois's third capital city in 1839, the move reflected a shift of power within the state. Located along the banks of the Mississippi River, downstate Kaskaskia was the first state capital after Illinois was admitted to the union in 1818. Just two years later the General Assembly was meeting in a more central location within the state's original counties—Vandalia.

Vandalia remained the seat of power for nearly two decades, but during that time many lawmakers, including a young Abraham Lincoln, petitioned for the capital to be moved again. During the 1836–37 session, the state legislator who later became the nation's sixteenth president introduced a bill that would move the capital to Springfield. Vandalia wasn't about to give up easily; a new brick statehouse was erected in hopes of keeping the legislature from moving closer to the geographical center of the state.

However, after four ballots Springfield received the most votes and power once again shifted northward in the state. Construction began on a building known today as the Old State Capitol, and the cupola-topped structure served as the seat of state government and center of Illinois politics until 1876.

Old State Capitol. Kevin Eatinger

House of Representatives chamber inside the Old State Capitol, 2019. Carol M. Highsmith, Library of Congress.

The cornerstone of this Greek Revival building, which is located in the town square, was laid in 1837. Architect John Francis Rague designed spaces for the state House and Senate, offices for the governor and other elected officials, a library, and chambers for the Illinois Supreme Court—all housed within a structure constructed of locally quarried yellow limestone.

Abraham Lincoln was often in the building, as an attorney and a politician. It was in Representative's Hall that Lincoln delivered his "House Divided" speech, where he declared his belief that a "government cannot endure permanently half slave and half free." This marked the beginning of Lincoln's campaign for the 1858 US Senate, a race that he lost to the "Little Giant," Stephen A. Douglas. However, in just two short years, Lincoln was nominated as the Republican candidate for president and used the governor's rooms in this building during the 1860 campaign.

Following Lincoln's inauguration in 1861, it was his former foe Douglas who spoke in Representative's Hall and urged the cheering crowd to put aside their differences in order to work to save the Union. And in the very same room, there occurred a somber event when the funeral train brought Lincoln's body back to Illinois after his 1865 assassination. He lay in state on a platform draped in velvet with silver tassels, as some seventy-five thousand mourners filed through to pay their respects.

In the years after Lincoln's death the state's population grew, as did its government, and within a few decades a larger building was needed. Construction began on a new statehouse in 1868, and although it was not completed until 1888, lawmakers moved in about halfway through the construction process. From 1876 until 1966, the Old State Capitol was then used as the county courthouse of Sangamon County, during which time the building was raised to accommodate another level. In 1966 a massive restoration project was undertaken. The structure was dismantled stone by stone and rebuilt; the interior was completely reconstructed to its appearance during Lincoln's time.

Nearly 150 years after Abraham Lincoln began his campaign, another candidate began a bid for the presidency. On a frigid ten-degree day in February 2007, Senator Barack Obama stood before the restored Old State Capitol and announced his candidacy for the White House. In a highly symbolic moment, Obama invoked the speech Lincoln gave here in 1858 condemning slavery—as he started his campaign to become the nation's first Black president.

Owen Lovejoy Residence, 1838–1864
Rural Route 3, East Peru Street, Princeton; (815) 879-9151; owenlovejoyhomestead.com

In the fall of 1838, a young man, "with black hair, broad shoulders, and peculiar expressive blue eyes" arrived in the small town on horseback. "He was alone," continued Nehemiah Matson, Bureau County's storyteller of pioneer days, "and a stranger without means, being in search of his future home, and came here by mere chance."

Born in Maine, Owen Lovejoy (1811–1864) ventured westward and settled in Alton, Illinois, to study theology under his brother. His lifelong passion was influenced by his brother's brutal death at the hands of a violent proslavery mob in 1837. Elijah Parish Lovejoy, then an abolitionist newspaper publisher, was killed on a moonlit night while trying to defend his printing press. As his brother lay dying, Owen vowed to carry on his work, believing slavery should be abolished.

How Lovejoy spent his time between the murder and relocating to Princeton in 1838 is not known. After arriving in the small town, which was known for abolitionist views, he became the minister of the Princeton Church and rented a room in this unassuming two-story home. The white clapboard house, then three-quarters of a mile east of town, had been built the previous year by Butler Denham. After a long illness Denham died, but not before instructing his wife to remarry in order to keep the 1,200-acre farm working. In 1843 Rev. Lovejoy married the widowed Eunice

Lovejoy Residence. Susan O'Connor

Denham, and their welcoming home came to be known as an important stop along one of the four routes on Illinois's Underground Railroad.

Lovejoy turned to politics to further this cause and twice ran for Congress as an abolitionist candidate on the Liberty Party ticket. He was unsuccessful; however, in 1854 he was elected to the Illinois State Legislature. He built a reputation as an eloquent and powerful speaker against slavery and was an early proponent of the emerging Republican Party. Two years later Lovejoy was elected (with Abraham Lincoln's support) as a Republican to the US House of Representatives, where he continued to be known for his fiery antislavery speeches.

Lovejoy faced prosecution several times for harboring enslaved people on their way north, as it was common knowledge that fugitives escaping from slavery to freedom were traveling on what was called the "Lovejoy Line," traveling over streams and through tall prairie grasses from Quincy to Galesburg to Princeton.

Lovejoy garnered national attention for a February 1859 speech in which he addressed his role in the Underground Railroad: "Owen Lovejoy . . . aids every fugitive that comes to his door and asks it. Proclaim it then from the housetops. Write it on every leaf that trembles in the forest, make it blaze from the sun at high noon . . . I bid you defiance in the name of my God!" This defiance of the Fugitive Slave Law marked a political difference with Lincoln, who for a time, distanced himself from Lovejoy.

Eventually the two became close, and Lovejoy was one of Lincoln's most ardent supporters. Lovejoy worked on legislation to end slavery in the District of Columbia and to prohibit slavery in all federal territories; in June 1862 Lincoln signed these into law. Owen Lovejoy did not live to see the full fruits of his efforts; he died in 1864, a year before the end of the Civil War. After hearing of Lovejoy's death President Lincoln wrote to John H. Bryant on May 30th: "it would scarcely wrong any other to say, he was my most generous friend."

Vachel Lindsay Residence, 1840
603 South Fifth Street, Springfield; (217) 782-6776; www2.illinois.gov/dnrhistoric/Experience/Sites; visitors by appointment only

The Poetry Foundation notes the importance of Vachel Lindsay; in the early twentieth century he was famous as a "traveling bard." Calling his public readings "Higher Vaudeville," Lindsay traversed through small towns of the Midwest delivering dramatic presentations of his poetry.

In 1878 Dr. Vachel Thomas Lindsay and his wife Catharine purchased this two-story clapboard house on the corner of Fifth and Edwards. But their new home, which was designated a National Historic Landmark in 1971, had an interesting history long before this family acquired the property and the connection was later reflected in the poet's work.

The house was built over thirty years earlier by Henry Dresser, who in 1844 sold his own house just a few blocks east to Abraham Lincoln. Ann Todd, the younger sister of Mary Todd Lincoln, and her husband Clark Moulton Smith purchased this house from Dresser in 1853. The Smiths often entertained the Lincolns here and this was but one of the many connections between the families.

Lincoln shopped at Smith's dry goods store. Needing a quiet place to compose his first inaugural address, he reportedly used a desk on the third floor of the store to write the speech. The Smith's gave a gala reception in their home the evening before the president-elect and Mrs. Lincoln departed for Washington. When Mary Todd Lincoln travelled to New York in January 1861, Smith accompanied her to help in the selection of clothing appropriate for the nation's first lady.

Decades later Nicholas Vachel Lindsay (1879–1931) was born in the northeast bedroom on the main floor of the house. When he was a young man, Nicholas's parents encouraged him to become a doctor. However, he struggled with the study of medicine and instead turned to poetry, publishing his first book, *Where Is Aladdin's Lamp*, in 1904. As his career progressed, Lindsay began to deliver dramatic public readings of his works.

Lindsay Residence. Kevin Eatinger

Lindsay witnessed the horrific 1908 race riot in Springfield that left several Black residents dead; it impacted him deeply. He produced a series of pieces that culminated in "*The Congo*" *and Other Poems*. These poems had a rhythmic structure based on African American speech patterns. In performance, the passages were exuberantly recited in a variety of voices ranging from a loud, deep bass to barely a whisper. Although reviewers noted the publication as "the single most interesting event in the American literary scene" at the time, Lindsay received criticism for a perceived racist portrayal of the subject matter.

In 1915 Lindsay wrote of another form of performance, the growing art of the silent film. The first section of his book *The Art of the Moving Picture* identifies different types of film forms. But the true impact of the work was Lindsay's enthusiasm for the future of moviemaking, although he did believe the addition of sound would reduce the impact of the visual images.

By the twenties, Lindsay's popularity waned as tastes changed; his folksy style belonged to an era long past. His works were generally a celebration of rural America in a century that witnessed a shift toward cities. Struggling physically and financially, Nicholas Vachel Lindsay committed suicide in December 1931.

His legacy recalls the town where he was born; Lindsay is most remembered for his 1914 work entitled *"Abraham Lincoln Walks at Midnight,"* a poem that describes Lincoln's ghostly return to their old neighborhood:

"It is portentous, and a thing of state
That here at midnight, in our little town
A mourning figure walks, and will not rest,
Near the old court-house pacing up and down."

Lyman Trumbull Residence, 1849–1863
1105 Henry Street, Alton; the house is a private residence and not open to the public

Described as a rather tall and spare gentleman with a sandy complexion and gold spectacles, distinguished senator Lyman Trumbull (1813–1896) became a friend of attorney Abraham Lincoln during his travels with the Illinois Circuit Court. At this time, they shared similar fundamental beliefs and would later become early members of the Republican Party.

Although Trumbull came to Illinois to practice law, he was appointed to succeed Stephen Douglas as secretary of state in 1840. He lost several subsequent elections as a Democratic candidate for governor and twice for Congress. By 1848 he was elected a justice of the Supreme Court of Illinois, and although known as a retiring and unassertive person, his careful opinions were thought to be among the soundest handed down by the court.

Trumbull purchased this Greek Revival house, now graced with dark green shutters, in 1849 and lived on the corner of Henry and Unions Streets until about 1863. Flanked by sidelights with an elliptical fanlight above, the front entrance opens into a central hall that divides the house into two wings. Except for the addition of a few rear rooms, and installation of modern heating, baths, and kitchens, the house remains much as it was when Lyman and Julia Trumbull lived here.

In 1855 Trumbull was elected to the US Senate when Lincoln (with a greater vote tally) yielded in order to break a deadlock, and he served for eighteen years. Although a senatorial opponent, Trumbull returned the favor and loyally supported Lincoln's candidacy for president in 1860. He campaigned for Lincoln and after five thousand people witnessed a debate between Abraham Lincoln and Stephen Douglas in 1858, Trumbull hosted a dinner for Lincoln at Alton's Franklin House Hotel.

After his election Lincoln relied on Trumbull, but they drifted apart once the president was inaugurated. Trumbull was never one of Lincoln's fervent supporters and the level of their unfriendliness is noted in a letter Trumbull's brother-in-law wrote to a friend. Trumbull had become alienated from the president: "Mr. Lincoln has not treated Mr. Trumbull as he should and Mr. T. said this morning, that he should not step inside the White House again during Mr. Lincoln's four years, unless he changed his course."

This estrangement happened despite connections between the two families that ran deep. Trumbull's first wife, Julia Jayne, was a bridesmaid for Mary Todd at her wedding; however, their friendship could not withstand politics, and the women's ties were severed after the 1855 Senate election.

Lincoln was questioned by his son Robert about the differences with Trumbull. "We agree perfectly, but we see things from a different point of view," replied the president. "I am in the White House looking down the Avenue, and Trumbull's in the Senate looking up."

Nonetheless, Lincoln and Trumbull were united in their belief in the immorality of slavery. Although Congress abolished slavery in the District of Columbia in 1862 and President Lincoln's Emancipation Proclamation ended the practice of slavery in rebellious states the following year, at war's end in 1865 the question of slavery had not been resolved at the national level. Lyman Trumbull co-authored the thirteenth amendment, ratified by the states on December 6, 1865, to abolish slavery "within the United States, or any place subject to their jurisdiction."

Abraham Lincoln Residence, 1849–1861
Eighth and Jackson Streets; (217) 492-4241; nps.gov/liho; visitor center, 426 South Seventh Street

On the rain-swept morning of February 11, 1861, the sixteenth president-elect of the United States stood on Springfield's train platform. Several thousand came to bid him well that Monday, and in a voice trembling with emotion, Abraham Lincoln addressed the crowd. "My friends, no one, not in my position can appreciate my feeling of sadness at this parting. To this place and the kindness of these people, I owe everything. Here I have lived a quarter of a century and have passed from a young to an old man. Here my children have been born and one is buried. I now leave, not knowing when, or whether ever, I may return."

Twenty-five years earlier Abraham Lincoln (1809–1865) first came to live in Springfield, but he was not a stranger to the town. As a young legislator Lincoln represented greater Sangamon County in the Illinois General Assembly, which then met in Vandalia. After Lincoln received his law license in the fall of 1836, the young attorney left the smaller town of New Salem—where he toiled as a postmaster, in a general store, as a boatman and rail-splitter—for a rapidly growing prairie city that offered more possibilities for his future.

When he arrived in Springfield on April 15, 1837, Lincoln had two saddlebags of belongings and very little money. He walked into Joshua Speed's store in search of bedclothes and came away with an offer to share the living quarters above the establishment. That same day Lincoln officially became the junior law partner of John

Lincoln Residence. Kevin Eatinger

Todd Stuart. Stuart and Lincoln met while the two served in the Black Hawk War and subsequently as opponents for a seat in the House of Representatives. Lincoln lost the election but gained a mentor and a connection to what his future would hold—Stuart was Mary Todd Lincoln's cousin.

Unlike Lincoln, Mary Todd came from a prominent family residing in the slavery state of Kentucky. In the fall of 1839, she moved to Springfield to live with her older sister Elizabeth, the wife of Ninian Wirt Edwards, whose family was active in local politics. Edwards served in the state House of Representatives, and Mary socialized with several young men and women who gathered at the Edwards's home. The group often included Stephen Douglas, Lyman Trumbull, and the young lawyer Abraham Lincoln.

Mary and Abraham became friendly, but their relationship had its share of ups and downs. Although facing pressure from her family members who felt the struggling country lawyer was not the right match, the couple decided to be married. The venue was to be a home that had been constructed in 1839 for the Episcopal minister, Reverend Charles Dresser. Upon hearing that news, the Edwards insisted the wedding be at their home, and on the evening of November 4, 1842, Rev. Dresser performed the marriage ceremony of twenty-three-year-old Mary to her suitor, thirty-three-year-old Abraham Lincoln.

For the first year of their marriage, the Lincolns lived in a single room on the second floor of the Globe Tavern, then located on Adams Street between Third and Fourth Streets. After their first son Robert Todd was born on August 1, 1843, the

Lincolns rented a three-room cottage at 214 South Fourth Street, between Adams and Monroe Streets, before purchasing the modest home of Reverend Dresser in the spring of 1844.

When Abraham Lincoln bought the house at the northeast corner of Eighth and Jackson Streets—the only house he would ever *own*—it was a white one-story structure with green shutters. The purchase price was fifteen hundred dollars, and for a time the family lived on a tight budget. Lincoln did many of the chores as he began to travel the Eighth Judicial Circuit. Lincoln created a name for himself as he traveled the sparsely settled area on horseback and in 1846 won election to the US House of Representatives as a Whig.

Both Lincoln and his house were works in progress. Structural evidence and Springfield tax records indicate that the Lincolns improved and expanded their home multiple times while they lived in it and apparently approved another renovation from the White House in 1863.

Initially projects were smaller; stoves were installed in the parlor rooms, a brick retaining wall in front of the home was constructed and the front wooden sidewalk was replaced with brick.

It was after Lincoln lost his 1855 bid for a US Senate seat to Lyman Trumbull that the most noticeable remodeling took place. By now they had buried one son, Eddie, and welcomed two more boys, Willie and Tad, into the family. That year the front of the house was raised to two full stories, creating bedroom space above, and a parlor was added at the rear of the house. The next remodeling of the house took place about 1856 when the rest of the house was raised to two full stories.

The last alterations the Lincolns undertook were small projects. These included tearing down the washing house in the backyard and adding a woodshed to the existing barn, completed in the latter part of 1859 and the beginning of 1860. In May, Lincoln was nominated by the Republican National Convention in Chicago to represent the party in the 1860 election.

Abraham Lincoln was elected president of the United States on November 6, 1860. At this time *Frank Leslie's Illustrated Newspaper* featured an article on the Lincoln home, writing, "The house in which a man of mark dwells is, like his handwriting, interesting, as to a certain degree indicating his character." The author continued to inform readers that rooms within the house were "simply and plainly fitted up" but not without "indications of taste and refinement."

With three short months to prepare for their move to Washington, DC, the Lincolns decided to rent their home rather than sell and placed their best belongings in storage for their eventual return. But on April 15, 1865, an assassin's bullet took the life of President Lincoln. Facing a lonely future, Mary Lincoln wrote she "could not bear to return to the scenes of the happiest times in my life without my family."

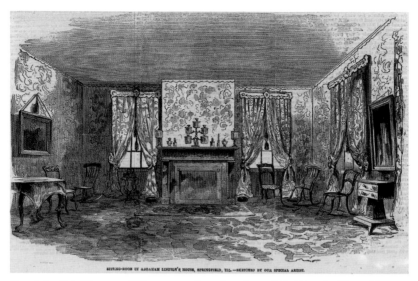

Frank Leslie's Illustrated Newspaper feat. drawings of the Lincoln Home Front Parlor and Sitting Room. Frank Leslie's Illustrated Newspaper. Courtesy of the Lincoln Home National Historic Site, National Park Service

Lincoln's only surviving son, Robert, donated the house to the State of Illinois in 1887 to be maintained and preserved for future generations. The National Park Service worked on the preservation and restoration of the home, along with the acquisition and restoration of the surrounding four-block neighborhood.

Ulysses S. Grant Residence, 1860–1880
500 Bouthillier Street, Galena; (815) 777-3310; granthome.com; entrance fee charged

In the early decades of the 1800s, Galena was a thriving town in northwest Illinois. The abundance of lead ore or "galena" in the hills along the Mississippi River was responsible for both the town's name and its prosperity. Ulysses Grant (1822–1885) arrived here in the spring of 1860, having completed military school at West Point Academy and fifteen years of military service. With little success outside the armed forces, he had hopes of reversing his economic misfortune by working for the family-owned store.

Grant and his wife Julia rented a modest brick home across the river, and he traveled considerably during the winter of 1860-61, visiting stores in the small towns across Wisconsin, Minnesota, and Iowa. But when war broke out that spring, Grant left his home to once again join the Army as commander of the unruly 21st Illinois Volunteer Infantry Regiment.

Proving a strong and capable leader, he was given significant responsibility of the Union forces, engineering the 1863 victory at Vicksburg that helped turn the tide of war. In March of the following year, Grant was appointed lieutenant general and commanded the Union Army until the war's end. When Robert E. Lee surrendered his troops to General Grant at the Appomattox Court House on April 9, 1865, Grant's legacy as a war hero was complete.

He returned to Galena in August, where the town turned out with a triumphal celebration. In addition to appreciating the parades and fireworks, Grant accepted generous presents. Local Republicans purchased a handsome house and presented it to the family. Designed in 1860 by William Dennison for former City Clerk Alexander J. Jackson, the house was typical of the Italianate style so popular at the time. Green shuttered windows were symmetrically placed on the brick façade, deep eaves were supported by ornate brackets, while a covered porch welcomed visitors.

Grant built on his military prowess, and as the Republican nominee for president in 1868 was elected to lead the country. After moving to Washington DC, the Grants rarely returned to Galena. When he visited the house for the last time in 1880, the local paper reported Grant found the house had been well taken care of in his absence; a new sidewalk had been laid, the trees were well-trimmed, and a new wash house had been built.

The Ulysses S. Grant, 2019. Carol M. Highsmith, Library of Congress.

Grant's children donated the house to the city of Galena as a memorial for their father, but it proved too costly for the city to maintain. The property was deeded to the state in 1931, and a major restoration project was undertaken two decades later. The house was returned to its 1868 appearance based on images that appeared in *Frank Leslie's Illustrated Newspaper* on November 14 of that year, filled with much of the family's furniture.

Abraham Lincoln Tomb, Oak Ridge Cemetery, 1868
1500 Monument Avenue, Springfield; (217) 789-2340; oakridgecemetery.org

Oak Ridge Cemetery has the distinction of being one of the most-visited cemeteries in the nation, second only to Arlington National Cemetery in the nation's capital. Almost one million visitors enter through the main gate annually, not only to pay respects to their deceased family and friends but to also visit the final resting place of the sixteenth president of our nation, Abraham Lincoln.

Prior to the mid-nineteenth century, formal burial in the United States was primarily restricted to interment on the grounds of a church or meetinghouse. As towns grew and populations increased, burial grounds moved to the outskirts of towns and cities. What then developed was a vision of a park-like cemetery based on English landscape gardening concepts. Located nearby, but in contrast to increasingly urban settings, cemeteries were consciously designed to provide a sanctuary where one could find adornment and beauty, solitude and quiet.

In 1855 the Springfield City Council acquired seventeen wooded acres north of the city for a cemetery. Mary and Abraham Lincoln attended the 1860 dedication ceremony a few days before his nomination for the presidency. Just five years later the remains of Lincoln and his son Willie (William Wallace Lincoln perished from typhoid in Washington DC in 1862) were transported from Washington DC and placed in the Oak Ridge receiving vault.

After Lincoln's assassination, fund-raising efforts began to create a monument appropriate for the slain president, and in 1868 a design competition was announced. Sculptor Larkin Goldsmith Mead Jr. was selected; his design featured an eighty-five-foot obelisk surrounded by statuary and was to be sited on six acres of land adjoining the cemetery.

Construction began in the fall of 1869 and continued for several years. The Lincolns' fourth and youngest son Tad was the first placed in the tomb, after his death in May 1871. The president's remains and those of his sons Willie and Eddie (Edward Baker Lincoln died in Springfield, 1852) were relocated to the structure in September of that year. Nine years and six months after Lincoln's death, the monument was formally dedicated in 1874, in a ceremony attended by President Ulysses Grant.

Lincoln's Tomb, the
final resting place of
martyred US president
Abraham Lincoln at
Oak Ridge Cemetery
in Springfield, Illinois,
"the second-most-visited
cemetery in the United
States, after Arlington
Cemetery in Virginia."
US, Sangamon County,
Springfield, Illinois,
2019. -10-10. Library
of Congress.
Carol M. Highsmith

Mary Todd Lincoln's final years were marked by declining health. She was confined to the Springfield residence of her sister Elizabeth Edwards and in July 1882 died in the home where she had married Lincoln. The former First Lady was laid to rest next to her husband and three of her sons; Robert Lincoln was buried at Arlington National Cemetery.

David Davis Residence, "Clover Lawn," 1870
1000 East Monroe Drive, Bloomington; (309) 828-1084;
daviddavismansion.org; donation suggested

In 1839 an ambitious young lawyer named David Davis (1815–1886) brought his new bride, Sarah Walker, from Massachusetts westward to Bloomington. Over the course of the next thirty-some years, Davis went from a circuit-riding lawyer to the nation's highest court. He maintained a longtime friendship with Abraham Lincoln and served as Lincoln's manager at the 1860 Republican nominating convention in Chicago. Two years later President Lincoln appointed Davis to the US Supreme

Court, where he served for fifteen years. He resigned from the court in 1877 when he was elected to the US Senate.

It was during his time on the Supreme Court that the Davises commissioned French-born architect Alfred H. Piquenard to design a residence indicative of their success and social standing. Well-known as one of the architects of the current Illinois State Capitol, Piquenard conceived an Italianate villa on a site near the outskirts of Bloomington. Largely supervised by Sarah Davis, the construction of the cream-colored structure—adorned with a distinctive tower, ornamental ironwork, and mansard roof—was completed in 1872.

Inside the elaborate thirty-six-room house visitors will find a collection that illustrates the life of a prosperous nineteenth-century family. The stately Davis mansion contained a remarkable number of conveniences unique for the time—gas lights, centralized steam heating, three bathrooms (the primary bathroom contained a bathtub with shower, washbasin, and flush toilet), a well-equipped kitchen, hot and cold running water in all the bedrooms, as well as a mechanical call-bell system.

The property was christened "Clover Lawn," and the ample grounds included a splendid garden patterned after classical Italian gardens of the seventeenth century and formal English gardens of the eighteenth century. The starburst design, pathways, and planting beds date from its creation in 1872 and contain an unusual amount of original plant material.

Their elaborate home and garden remained in the family for three succeeding generations, providing a focal point for the social, cultural, and political life of Bloomington. The house, and nearly everything within, was donated to the State of Illinois in 1960.

Davis Residence. Kevin Eatinger

URBAN DEVELOPMENT

ILLINOIS 1869–1900

Hog Butcher for the World
Tool Maker, Stacker of Wheat
Player with Railroads and the Nation's Freight Handler;
Stormy, husky, brawling,
City of the Big Shoulders

—CARL SANDBURG, CHICAGO, 1916

The prize-winning bull "Sherman," Union Stockyard Gate. Kevin Eatinger

Rock Island Arsenal, Building No. 1, 1869
Gillespie Avenue between Terrace Drive & Hedge Lane, Rock Island;
(309) 782-5890 (museum); arsenalhistoricalsociety.org

The last time the fierce Sauk war chief Black Hawk appeared in public was at a Fourth of July celebration in Fort Madison, Iowa. He spoke briefly that 1837 day: "A few summers ago I was fighting against you. I did wrong, perhaps, but that is past— it is buried—let it be forgotten. Rock River was a beautiful country. . . . I fought for it—it is now yours—keep it as we did."

The country did not heed his advice; as thousands of settlers came to northern Illinois, the terrain was altered in a relatively short time. Domesticated crops replaced prairie grasses and woodlands, while the building of canals, railroads, towns, and cities transformed the landscape.

The Rock Island Arsenal is located on a three-mile-long island in a gentle bend of the Mississippi River, in Sauk territory between Davenport, Iowa, and Rock Island, Illinois. The 946 acres that were once the summer camp of Native Americans became home to Fort Armstrong in 1816, one of a chain of small, isolated defense

Rock Island Barracks, Illinois. Rock Island, Illinois, C. Speidel, 1864.
Library of Congress

Rock Island Arsenal, Building No. 1, 1933. Historic American Buildings Survey, Library of Congress

posts at the western boundary of the country. In 1832 the fort was used as military headquarters during the Black Hawk War and abandoned four years later.

With the destruction of the federal armory at Harper's Ferry in April 1861 and the start of the Civil War, the need for a new, secure federal arsenal was apparent. The island's strategic location, both in terms of its ability to resist invasion as well as its favorable access to river and rail transportation, made it attractive to serve as a federal installation.

In July 1862 Congress approved the construction of an arsenal at Rock Island, and the site became one of the largest military construction projects of the nineteenth century. Today Rock Island is home to the First Army headquarters and is the largest government-owned weapons manufacturing arsenal in the country. In addition to manufacturing weaponry, the arsenal provides logistics and base support for the Armed Forces.

Visitor sites include the Arsenal Museum, the Confederate Cemetery (most of the nearly two thousand Confederate prisoners held in camps died from disease), ten workshops constructed of Joliet limestone, the clock tower, gatehouse, and officers' quarters along the river. Of those quarters, the limestone house built by Brigadier General Thomas J. Rodman is most impressive. Quarters One is a massive, twenty-thousand-square-foot, lavishly detailed building—representing the largest single residence held by the Army and considered the second-largest government residence, next to the White House.

By October 1871 the structure of Quarters One was almost complete, yet something was missing from the completion of this marvelous project: Rodman himself. He died four months before the Italianate Villa–style structure was fully complete, and the funeral service marked the first public event inside the parlors of Quarters One. Rodman is buried at Rock Island National Cemetery. His grave is flanked by three Rodman Guns, which were used in coastal defenses around the United States for many years.

Quarters One has been the home of every senior officer assigned to Rock Island. Today portraits of those thirty-eight officers line the main stairway, but due to a variety of reasons the US Army decided in 2006 that Quarters One would no longer be used as housing.

Riverside Historic District, 1869
Riverside; no hours; no admission charged

As Chicago grew in the years after the Civil War, it became an increasingly congested place to live. Businessmen sensed lucrative opportunities by providing people of means with an alternative to the congestion of the city, made possible by the growing number of train lines that provided access to suburbs developing to the north, south, and west.

In April 1869, the Riverside Improvement Company was established and charged with the goal of building a bucolic alternative to city living. The investors purchased a parcel of sixteen hundred acres of land located nine miles west of the heart of the business district. Its location along the Des Plaines River provided a name and pastoral setting, while easy access to the railroad line ensured a swift commute to the city.

The improvement company arranged for the infrastructure—water, sewer, and gas—and commissioned the nation's most influential and admired landscape firm of the time to create the plans for the village. Frederick Law Olmsted and Calvert Vaux, responsible for the design of New York City's Central Park, started with a blank canvas of farmland along the winding river.

Olmsted and Vaux were influenced by Andrew Jackson Downing, a well-known nurseryman and landscape gardener. Downing promoted the idea that homeowners should take pride in the landscape surrounding their houses, and that the ideal

Riverside Water Tower. Susan O'Connor

home was one that combined the healthful aspects of country living with the cultural aspects of urban settings.

As envisioned by Olmsted, the planned community of Riverside became a series of curvilinear streets that wound across each other, combined with green areas along the meandering river. The result was a picturesque setting that stood in stark contrast

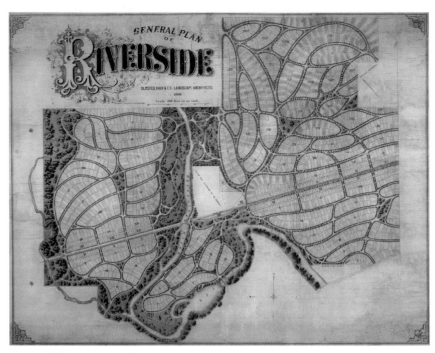

General Plan of Riverside. Courtesy of the Olmsted Society

to Chicago's rigid grid layout. Completing the vision of this self-contained village, the plans included a town square with a surrounding business district.

The Riverside Water Tower was one of the very first projects the founders undertook, to ensure a clean, adequate water supply. Located near the center of the planned development, the design would be a striking identifying symbol for the new community, while its observation platform allowed potential buyers to have a bird's-eye view of the community.

Before their idyllic plan could be fully executed, the developers declared bankruptcy. In the dry fall of 1871, a massive fire burned most of the central business district of Chicago and a financial panic followed. While some chose to rebuild in the city, an outmigration to the suburbs was underway. Before long the development gained momentum again and noted architect William Le Baron Jenney completed the plans, after Olmsted's firm resigned over a fee dispute. Jenney is most remembered as the architect of the first steel-framed skyscraper, the Home Insurance Building, built in 1884. But years earlier Jenney oversaw the completion of Olmsted's vision for Riverside.

In addition to his supervisory role, Jenney designed the town's 124-room hotel (destroyed by fire 1932) and many of the first homes, including his own at 200

Nutall Road (destroyed by fire in 1910). Other notable architects of the day, such as Frank Lloyd Wright and Louis Sullivan, designed houses in the community. Today the gently curving streets, gas lamps, and tranquil parks evoke what an "ideal" suburb looked like in the nineteenth century. Riverside was designated a National Historic Landmark in 1970.

Grosse Point Light Station, 1873
2601 Sheridan Road, Evanston; (847) 328-6961; grossepointlighthouse.net; grounds are open to the public free of charge year-round; entrance fee charged for lighthouse tours

Native Americans recognized the beauty of this site along the lake; the Potawatomi called it "Eyebrow of the Beauty" for the shape of the land when seen from the water. Early French explorers also noted the topography and used the name Grosse Pointe, meaning a great point or promontory. In those years the point was a more distinct outcropping than it is today—years of development and landfill have altered the shoreline.

As Chicago grew dramatically in size and importance due to its strategic Midwest location, traffic on Lake Michigan increased. Mariners had to be particularly careful when approaching or leaving the city's harbor, as in various locations near the shore there are shallow areas of water (known as shoals) that played havoc with vessels.

Late in the evening of September 7, 1860, the steamship *Lady Elgin* left Chicago crowded with some four hundred people on their return trip to Milwaukee. It was a warm end to summer, and further out on the lake music still played in the forward cabin of the charter at two thirty the next morning. Thunderstorms blew up, visibility lessened, and high waves followed, but the dancing and gaiety continued onboard. As weather conditions declined the lumber schooner *Augusta*, overloaded and barely lit, rammed the *Lady Elgin*. Panic ensued as water poured in, and the vessel broke apart and sank within thirty minutes.

Fleeing the badly damaged *Lady Elgin*, passengers jumped, or were thrown into the water by high waves, and clung to anything that floated. By daybreak the shore near the Grosse Point shoal was lined with people helping, when possible, but frightfully watching as survivors battled the elements in their attempts to reach land. Nearly four hundred people perished.

The sinking of the *Lady Elgin* was the greatest tragedy to strike Lake Michigan's waters. The tragedy spurred the nearby city of Evanston to petition Congress for a lighthouse on Grosse Point, but the Civil War delayed the project.

Then in 1871, not long after the Great Chicago Fire, Congress formally authorized construction of a lighthouse.

Grosse Point Lighthouse. Kevin Eatinger

Construction began in 1872 under the watchful eye of Orlando Metcalf Poe, a US Army officer and engineer who supervised the building of many early lighthouses on the Great Lakes. On March 1, 1874, traditionally the start of the inland shipping season, the Grosse Point Lighthouse sent its welcome beacon of light over the waters of Lake Michigan for the first time. The lead lighthouse marking the approach to Chicago stands 113-feet tall and its beam of light could be seen up to twenty-one miles over the lake in good conditions, serving both to warn ships of shallow waters around the point and to guide the way toward the port of Chicago.

Keepers' Quarters. Kevin Eatinger

In addition to the tower, the light station includes the keepers' quarters—a duplex building with an aboveground passageway that leads to the light tower. The structure is detailed in a style typical of the Italianate period in American architecture, and the brick duplex contains two distinct living quarters designed as mirror images of one another.

At its height of operation, Grosse Point Lighthouse required three keepers and a day laborer to keep the light and fog signals in top condition. In 1934 the station was automated and decommissioned. Its beacon was extinguished during the Second World War but relit in 1946, and the site remains operational under the supervision of the Lighthouse Park District.

Second Presbyterian Church, 1874–1901
1936 South Michigan Avenue, Chicago; (312) 225-4951; 2ndpresbyterian.org

Chicago flourished after the end of the Civil War; its population grew to over three hundred thousand by 1870. Lured by brisk economic growth and anticipated prosperity, thousands arrived every year to take advantage of the opportunities Chicago had to offer.

Their dreams of success were interrupted on a warm October evening in 1871 when, after a hot and dry summer, a fire began in Patrick and Catherine O'Leary's barn on the Near South Side. Fueled by densely packed frame houses and wooden sidewalks, and encouraged by a strong wind from the southwest, the fire quickly spread. Despite firefighters' efforts to contain it, the massive blaze moved steadily to the northeast. By the time the inferno reached the central business district, masonry walls of commercial buildings that were supposed to be fireproof tumbled to the ground. After three days rain began to fall, and the great fire died out roughly four and a half miles from the O'Leary barn, leaving the entire business district in ruins.

One of the architectural treasures lost to the inferno was affectionately known as the "Spotted Church," for its limestone exterior contained tar deposits that gave the stone a spotted appearance. Architect James Renwick Jr. of New York was the architect of the structure. Renwick was just twenty-five when he won his first commission in 1843 to build New York's Grace Episcopal Church. That Gothic Revival building brought him renown, and he designed the spotted sanctuary in much the same style.

The church trustees selected a new site south of the commercial center of the city. Renwick again selected to design the new edifice at the northwest corner of Michigan Avenue and Cullerton. By then his fame had grown to include such commissions as the original building of the Smithsonian (the Castle) in Washington DC and St. Patrick's Cathedral in New York.

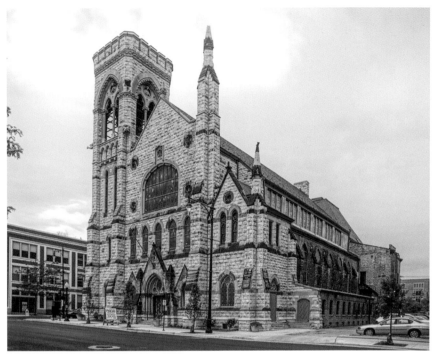

Second Presbyterian Church. Kevin Eatinger

Renwick's design for the new church was inspired by early English Gothic houses of worship, with a high-pitched gable roof, a rose window on the east wall, and a dramatic bell tower anchoring the corner. The interior was also in the Gothic style, with pointed arches leading to side aisles.

When construction on the present building began in 1872, the neighborhood around the church was the most exclusive residential district in the city. Prairie Avenue was lined with elegant mansions housing the business and social leaders of the city, many of whom also worshipped at Second. In the latter decades of the nineteenth century, members of the church included such prominent citizens as Robert Todd Lincoln, George Pullman, George Armour, and William Blair.

In early spring 1900, fire destroyed the interior of the new church but this time the stone walls survived intact. Howard Van Doren Shaw, a lifelong member of the church and a trustee, was selected as the architect for the project. Shaw chose not to recreate the original Gothic Revival interior; instead, he designed the interior in the Arts & Crafts style, focusing on unity of design and hand craftsmanship. The sanctuary has been virtually unchanged since it was rebuilt in 1901, except for the addition of stunning memorial windows made by William Morris & Company, Tiffany Studios, McCully & Miles, and Louis J. Millet.

Nave, redesigned by Howard van Doren Shaw. Kevin Eatinger

By the 1920s the neighborhood around the church had changed dramatically. Wealthy families had moved away, and many of their mansions were converted for business use or served as boarding houses. Others were simply boarded up or torn down. Michigan Avenue evolved from an elegant residential street into "Motor Row," with some one hundred buildings housing automobile dealerships and other industry-related businesses.

In the ensuing years the congregation declined steadily, and various ministers advocated abandoning the building and moving elsewhere in the city. By the late 1960s, church membership was under seventy parishioners. Serious discussions were undertaken as to the future of the church, and the decision was made to keep the doors open. Extensive renovations to the building were made with the hope and belief that the church and neighborhood would thrive once again. And such it has.

Hegeler-Carus Residence, 1876
1307 Seventh Avenue, LaSalle; (815) 224-6543; hegelercarus.org

When the Great Chicago Fire tore through the heart of the city in 1871, most of the works conceived by architect William W. Boyington were lost, although his Water Tower and Pumping Station on Michigan Avenue were spared and remain beloved city landmarks today. However, about one hundred miles southwest of the city is

Hegeler Carus Foundation. Cynthia Waddick, Executive Director / April Murphy, Photographer

another remarkable example of Boyington's vocation that can be seen in the river town of LaSalle, the western terminus of the Illinois and Michigan Canal.

In 1856 Edward Hegeler (1835-1910) left his native Germany and came to America with his business partner in search of opportunity. With dreams of establishing a zinc manufacturing company, Hegeler and Frederick Matthiessen found an optimum site for such an operation in LaSalle. Abundant coal deposits offered fuel to purify the zinc, while the Illinois Central Railroad and I & M Canal promised two means of transporting the product to market. The zinc was shipped across the country to be made into ice-box liners, gutters, and galvanized nails. By 1880 theirs was the largest such business in the country.

As their success grew, so did the family; Boyington was commissioned to design a sixteen-thousand-square-foot mansion on a bluff overlooking the scenic river valley. Constructed between 1874 and 1876, the architect created a formal Second Empire–style house with a distinctive mansard roof. Cement parging was used to create a smooth exterior appearance—a quiet backdrop for the dramatic double-curve stairway leads to a second-level veranda.

The elaborate interiors were designed by August Fiedler. Like Boyington, much of his interior design and furniture has been lost; this house is the largest and the most intact surviving example of his work. Thanks to the family's long occupancy of the house, much of the original interior decoration is 145 years old: extraordinary parquet floors, elaborate ceiling decorations in the public rooms, large mirrors,

Hegeler-Carus Foundation. Cynthia Waddick, Executive Director / April Murphy, Photographer

extensive built-ins, and rich woodwork. More than 85 percent of the family's furnishings remain in place to this day.

An intellectual as well as a businessman, Hegeler founded the Open Court Publishing Company in 1887. This was one of the first academic presses in the country, and the privately held company published hundreds of books and articles that were very influential in the fields of comparative religion, philosophy, science, and mathematics.

Hegeler hired a fellow German, Dr. Paul Carus, to be the managing editor. He ended up as much more, for Carus married the family's eldest daughter Mary in 1888. For the next thirty years Carus ran a highly successful publishing operation out of the ground floor of the mansion. And Mary was successful in her own right; she was the first woman to graduate from the University of Michigan in engineering (1882). Mary Carus followed her father's footsteps, attending the School of Mines in Germany and then returned to LaSalle to run the family business, acting as president for three terms at a time when she did not even have the right to vote.

The Carus descendants occupied the mansion until 2004; it is now operated by the Hegeler-Carus Foundation.

Union Stock Yard Gate, c.1879
850 West Exchange Avenue, Chicago; no hours, no admission charged

Written in 1916, Carl Sandburg's poem "Chicago" became one of the best-known works of twentieth-century American literature. This poem famously described Chicago as the "City of the Big Shoulders," celebrating its role as the industrial capital of the country. But the poem begins with another of the city's vast enterprises that defined the city for generations: "Hog Butcher for the World."

The sprawling Union Stock Yard opened on Christmas Day 1865 on the city's south side. On a square mile of city turf bounded by 39th Street south to 47th and Halsted west to Ashland Avenue, the operation processed two million animals annually by 1870. By 1890 the number had increased to nine million, and some forty thousand people were employed at the height of business.

The lone remaining symbol of the vast stockyards is a rugged limestone gateway that was erected about a decade after the facility opened. Located at Exchange and Peoria Streets, the muscular structure is attributed to the noted architectural firm of Burnham & Root. Centered over the limestone arch is a steer thought to represent a prize-winning bull, "Sherman." The animal was named for one of the founders of the Union Stock Yard and Transit Company, John B. Sherman, who was also architect Daniel Burnham's father-in-law.

Union Stock Yard Gate. Kevin Eatinger

Charles Rascher, The Great Union Stock Yards of Chicago, Illinois, ca. 1878. Chicago: Published by Walsh & Co. Library of Congress

The impact of the Union Stock Yard on the city and labor was enormous. The site was a bloody hub where thousands of animals were slaughtered daily on a "disassembly" line. There were ongoing struggles between workers and management, ethnic conflict, and poor labor conditions. The dangerous and unsanitary conditions were immortalized in another work of literature, Upton Sinclair's classic novel *The Jungle*.

Sinclair described the exploitation of immigrants working in dangerous and filthy conditions for very low wages. The livestock was poorly fed, overcrowded, and often sickly. Disease-ridden animals, and others not legal to butcher, were heavily processed into packed meat products. Although *The Jungle* was considered a work of fiction, inspectors found that the conditions described so graphically in the novel were, in fact, rampant at the stockyards. Sweeping legislation protecting worker and consumer health and safety followed soon after.

Over time, improvements in transportation made it more efficient and cheaper for meat producers to process livestock where the animals were raised. After 106 years, the meat-processing center of the country closed in 1971.

John J. Glessner Residence, 1885–1886
**1800 South Prairie Avenue, Chicago; glessnerhouse.org;
312-326-1480; admission charged**

During the latter half of the eighties, the influence of Boston architect Henry Hobson Richardson (1838–1886) was widespread. Despite its medieval origins, "Richardsonian Romanesque" has been accepted as an original and highly influential American architectural style. Richardson used natural materials such as rustic stone and implemented Romanesque principles of construction to create robust architectural compositions. Conveying a sense of strength and power, this massive style was far too expensive for the typical homeowner and was reserved for the upper class.

John Jacob Glessner (1843–1936) had strength and power in his own right and joined the city's movers and shakers on exclusive Prairie Avenue. Glessner was a self-made man who arrived in Chicago in 1870 with a limited education but great ambition. Warder, Bushnell & Glessner found a strong market in Illinois for their company's farm product, the Champion reaper, in a field dominated by such storied names as McCormick, Harvester, and Deering. After the turn of the century Glessner was instrumental in the merger of his company with his competitors. Today, the formidable enterprise is globally known as International Harvester.

Glessner Residence. Kevin Eatinger

First floor stairhall, south. Historic American Buildings Survey Photocopy c. 1923 from J. J. Glessner *The Story of a House*. Library of Congress

Prairie Avenue was one of the most exclusive addresses in Chicago when this house was built, counting over twenty millionaires living on a four-block stretch of the street. One guidebook published around the time of the 1893 Columbian Exposition described it as the most expensive street in America west of New York's Fifth Avenue.

Glessner had already purchased the lot when he first met with Richardson, and the architect immediately addressed its inherent problem: how to get light and air into a building at the northern end of a city block. To accomplish this, the exterior walls were pushed nearly to the lot line and an interior courtyard was placed facing south.

Richardson did not live to see the house under construction; he died three weeks after completing the design of the residence. Afterward, only one change was made to his creation, but it was a major one. Richardson specified a granite base with pink Georgia marble above; however, after John and Frances Glessner visited a north side house using that very material, they authorized a change to granite for the entire street elevation.

Although the house contains more than seventeen thousand square feet, there are no large open spaces—this is the antithesis of the Prairie Style yet to come. Eleven rooms often have a centrally placed fireplace and are connected. Three bedrooms were for family use, two for guests and eight more required for the servants who cared for the residence. Although it was wired for electricity when the house was built, light came from gas fixtures for the first five or six years the Glessners lived here. There was no infrastructure to provide electricity to the neighborhood; the entire house was electrified in time for the much-anticipated World's Fair of 1893.

Prairie Avenue began a steep decline after the turn of the century. Fashion turned to the development of the Gold Coast on the city's north side, and the avenue quickly fell out of favor as business encroached on the once-regal houses. By 1910 many of the mansions lining the avenue had been converted to rooming houses or repurposed as factories.

Clearly worried for the fate of their home, in 1924 the Glessners signed a deed that would give the house to the Chicago Chapter of the American Institute of Architects (AIA) upon their deaths. It provided that the residence be used solely to promote architecture, art and science, and to always be known as Glessner House.

The AIA described Richardson's creation as his "finest urban residence'" and "a dwelling of extraordinary distinction." It is currently a museum and the centerpiece of the historic Prairie Avenue District, designated in the 1970s to showcase the few remaining Prairie Avenue houses.

Fort Sheridan Historic District, 1889
County Street, Waukegan; fortsheridan.com, grounds are open to the public

Located twenty-five miles north of Chicago, Fort Sheridan was an important turn-of-the-nineteenth-century military post set among prosperous suburbs. Situated along the lakefront, the 714-acre complex was planned and constructed during a period of transition in national military policy. Temporary frontier posts were closed, and permanent garrisons of troops were established at strategic points throughout the United States.

Fort Sheridan Water Tower. Susan O'Connor

The origins of the fort also had strong local influences. Following the 1886 Haymarket Affair, the Commercial Club of Chicago purchased the land and donated it to the federal government. Their hope was the army would accept the gift and use the site as one of the strategic locations. The army would then be available to provide troops for the protection of property and the suppression of further labor unrest.

Fort Sheridan, general quarters. Susan O'Connor

Commanding general and Civil War hero Philip H. Sheridan supported the plan, and President Grover Cleveland named the post in his honor.

Designed by the nationally significant firm of Holabird & Roche, the architects designed sixty-six distinctive buff-color buildings built around a central parade ground. The southern side of the grounds provides a stunning focal point, a 167-foot-high water tower flanked by two dormitories that stretch more than a thousand feet in length. The post also included officers' quarters, a hospital, a pumping station warehouse, a morgue, and, demonstrating the importance of horses and mules to the army, stables.

In its history, troops from Fort Sheridan responded to labor unrest only once, during the Pullman strikes of 1894. The post was the site for training, administration, and mobilization of forces from the Spanish-American War through the Second World War, when over a half million men and women were processed at the fort.

Ninety-four buildings, including those originally designed by Holabird & Roche, were designated a National Historic Landmark in 1984. After the army post was closed in 1993, the Fort Sheridan Joint Planning Commission was formed to develop an adaptive reuse plan. The Army Reserve continues to use about ninety acres; the remaining property is divided between a golf course and a variety of residential developments.

SOCIAL REFORM

ILLINOIS 1880–1925

Liberty produces wealth, and wealth destroys liberty.
—HENRY DEMAREST LLOYD

Administration Clock Tower Building, Pullman National Monument.
Susan O'Connor

Pullman Historic District, 1880
11141 South Cottage Grove Avenue, Chicago;
(773) 468-9310; nps.gov/pull

Representing the concepts of both urban development and social reform is the town of Pullman, located on the city's far south side. Architect Solon Spencer Beman (1853–1914) created a model town for railroad car magnate George Pullman (1831–1897), which later became a focal point of classic labor struggles.

Pullman believed it would be smart business to provide an improved standard of living for his workers. According to the National Park Service, the town of Pullman was conceived as a total planned community with the intent to attract the most skilled workforce to his plant and to insulate workers from the social ills plaguing industrialized cities across the country. The resulting community provided an orderly, efficient environment that included housing and community facilities far superior to what was available elsewhere.

Housing was designed for mixed economic classes and rented to workers who could never afford to purchase a similar home. Utilities and indoor plumbing were included in the rent, and housing was available in a range of options depending on one's position. A variety of shops and services, schools, a church, and a hotel—along with lushly landscaped streets, parks and even a lake—put the accommodations far above the standard of the day.

The Pullman Palace Car Company began in 1867 with the idea that train travel should be more than just comfortable—it should be elegant. When a luxurious Pullman car was built and leased to a railroad, it was staffed with highly trained porters. The porters were often recently freed enslaved persons, whom Pullman judged to be skilled in serving travelers and willing to work for low wages. Before long the Pullman Rail Car Company was the largest employer of Blacks in the country.

The planned community was not intended for the porters, but to attract skilled workers, cabinet makers, and upholsterers—mostly white immigrants from Europe. But they found a society that went beyond uplift and veered into social control. Limitations on their freedom coincided with a severe economic downturn in 1894 and led to social unrest.

Problems were exacerbated when workers became dissatisfied with layoffs and a reduction in wages, while rents in the company town remained firm. Under the leadership of Eugene Debs, workers founded a union and went on strike, essentially crippling railroad service nationwide. For a time, the strike went on peacefully; however, President Cleveland saw the boycott as a threat to the nation's mail service and ordered federal troops stationed at Fort Sheridan to Chicago to quell the uprising. Riots, shootings, and fires followed.

Hotel Florence, Pullman. Susan O'Connor

For the railroad officials and executives of the meatpacking industry who relied upon the railroads and backed Pullman's position, this was a frightening time. During the hot summer months of 1894 blazing fires at Pullman lit the night skies. Thousands of federal and state troops were in the vicinity when Debs and other leaders were arrested. The strike continued until early August, when the Pullman works reopened.

Debs was charged with obstructing commerce, and the case worked its way to the nation's highest court. Although defended by Clarence Darrow and the venerable eighty-one-year-old Lyman Trumbull, the Supreme Court ruled against Debs. However, the Pullman strike demonstrated the vast power of a unified national labor union and the willingness of the federal government to support capitalists against organized labor.

The 1981 bi-level Amtrack Superliner was the last Pullman car the company produced. The restoration of the Pullman Clock Tower and Administration Building was announced in September 2020 as part of thirty-four million dollars in restoration work happening in the historic district. President Barack Obama made the district a national landmark in 2015, citing Pullman "typifies many of the economic, social, and design currents running through American life in the late 19th and early 20th century, yet it is unlike any other place in the country."

Hull-House, 1889
**800 South Halsted Street, Chicago; (312) 413-5353;
hullhousemuseum.org; a donation is suggested**

Charles Jared Hull (1820–1889) was a Chicago real estate developer, best remembered today for the Italianate-style house he built in 1856 near present-day South Halsted and Polk Streets. Upon his death and to the dismay of his nephews, Hull left his entire estate, including this property and 2 million dollars, to his cousin Helen Culver (1832-1925). Almost immediately Ms. Culver, a schoolteacher, began to consider plans for a use of the assets.

In the latter decades of the nineteenth century, settlement houses arose in response to problems created by urbanization, industrialization, and immigration. Jane Addams (1860–1935) and Ellen Starr Gates (1859–1940) began their work the year of Hull's death. Recognizing the value and promise of their work, Culver offered Hull's house rent-free to the founders. Even though Addams and Gates originally named their settlement Chicago Toynbee Hall (after a settlement house in East London), the name "Hull" stuck.

Hull-House was founded to support the disadvantaged citizens of Chicago's Near West Side neighborhood. Located amid a densely populated urban neighborhood favored by Italian, Irish, German, Greek, and Jewish immigrants, the endeavor began with modest goals; however, the role of Hull-House quickly grew beyond what either founder could have imagined.

Hull-House, south façade. Kevin Eatinger

In addition to Addams and Gates, Hull-House supporters included many influential Chicagoans who contributed to a powerful reform movement. Among the projects that Hull-House helped launch were the Immigrants' Protective League and the Juvenile Protective Association. Their efforts led to protective legislation for women and children in 1893. The strength of Hull-House's endeavors went nationwide with the creation of the Federal Children's Bureau (1912) and the passage of a federal child labor law (1916).

By the 1920s demographics of the area surrounding Hull-House changed as African Americans and Mexican immigrants began to put down roots in the neighborhood. They too came to participate in programs offered by Hull-House: kindergarten and day care facilities for the children of working mothers, an employment bureau, libraries, English and citizenship classes, and theater, music and art classes.

As a result of her work, Jane Addams was awarded the Nobel Peace Prize in 1931. Of the settlement complex's original thirteen buildings, nearly all were demolished to make way for the construction of the University of Illinois at Chicago Circle campus during the 1960s. Today the museum is comprised of the Hull home and the Residents' Dining Hall. As to Hull-House supporter Helen Culver, the New York Times remarked that her death "closed a career that had been remarkable for over a half century." She was a successful executive at a time "when women in business were almost unknown."

Haymarket Martyrs' Monument, 1886–1893
863 Plaines Avenue, Forest Park; (708) 366-1900

Historians consider Haymarket one of the seminal events in the history of American labor. On May 1, 1886, close to forty thousand workers in the city took part in nationwide demonstrations in support of an eight-hour workday. Chicago became the center of the movement for workers' rights, and the International Working Peoples' Association (IWPA) played a principal role in organizing the nearly 250,000 May Day strikers demanding a shorter work week and equal pay.

Members of the IWPA planned a rally at Haymarket Square, on the corner of Des Plaines Avenue and Randolph Street, to protest police brutality against striking workers. Late in the evening of Tuesday, May 4, 1886, at the close of a long day of speeches in support of the strikers, something flew over the heads of those in the audience and into the middle of the police stationed there. A terrifying explosion rattled the street and shattered windows in the surrounding Near West Side blocks. A bomb had been thrown; for a moment there was nothing but bewildered silence, then other officers drew their guns and fired into the crowd.

Haymarket Martyrs' Monument. Kevin Eatinger

Seven police officers and an unknown number of civilians were killed immedi-ately, in what became known as the Haymarket tragedy. Six more policemen died as a result of their wounds. In the well-publicized legal proceedings that followed, eight anarchists were tried for murder. Although the prosecution conceded that none of the defendants had thrown the bomb, four men were executed and one committed suicide while in prison.

No cemetery within the Chicago city limits would allow the martyrs to be buried on their grounds, so the remains were placed in Waldheim (now Forest Home) Cemetery. There was some reluctance, but the cemetery's policy accepted everyone regardless of race, ethnicity, or politics.

Dedicated on June 23, 1893, the Haymarket Martyrs' Monument consists of a sixteen-foot-high granite shaft atop a two-stepped base on which stand two bronze figures. Designed by sculptor Albert Weinert, the female figure represents Justice placing a wreath on the head of a fallen worker. The bottom of the monument features the final words of accused anarchist August Spies: "The day will come when our silence will be more powerful than the voices you are throttling today."

Henry Demarest Lloyd Residence, 1880–1903
830 Sheridan Road, Winnetka; the private residence is not open to the public

One would not typically think of the well-to-do North Shore suburb of Winnetka as home to Socialists. However, journalist, lecturer, writer and reformer Henry Demarest Lloyd (1847–1903) lived here while supporting economic and social reform during the excesses of America's Gilded Age.

Educated in law and experienced in politics, H.D. Lloyd turned to writing in order to influence public opinion. In 1881, he published an exposé on the railroad monopolies and Standard Oil Company in *Atlantic Monthly*. Entitled "Story of a Great Monopoly," the piece caused such a sensation that the issue had to be reprinted six times and earned him the title of "muckraker" for his exposure of injustices and abuses in American society—"When monopolies succeed, the people fail."

Nearly a decade earlier, Lloyd came from New York to join the editorial staff of the *Chicago Tribune*. For nearly thirteen years he worked as an editor for various departments. His witty and piercing editorials on behalf of reform in business and government, and his views against child labor and for the eight-hour workweek, attracted national attention.

The stint at the *Tribune* also benefitted Lloyd personally. He married the boss's daughter, Jesse Bross, on Christmas Day 1873. A passionate and independent woman, Jesse was well educated and regarded her husband's work and causes as the focus of their life together.

Lloyd's attack on local injustices began with the arrest and trial of the anarchists in the Haymarket bombing in May 1886. While having no sympathy for the use of violence in labor disputes, Lloyd pleaded for the anarchists and was influential in

Lloyd Residence and "Everyman." Susan O'Connor

securing commutations for two of them. His health became precarious following the executions of the others and Lloyd's criticism of the trial judge led to being socially ostracized by Chicago's elite.

Eventually his father-in-law William Bross concurred, removed Lloyd from a position at the *Tribune* and then disinherited his own daughter. Henry and Jesse left the pressures of the city and retreated to the relative quiet of the North Shore. On a tree-shaded village street within sight of the lake, they found a derelict country inn that they purchased and restored. Built about 1855, "Wayside" became the family's home.

Never wanting to live the average life of a housewife, Jesse worked with her husband to engage social activists; college presidents, union organizers and Hull-House leaders visited their home. Lloyd continued his attacks on the country's great monopolies, but also found the time to cover other diverse topics including food legislation, African American land ownership, preventive medicine, and immigration.

Now located on the west side of Sheridan Road, their rambling house is across the street from Lloyd Park, a public space extending toward a sandy beach that was previously part of the estate. The two-and-a-half-story brick structure has been altered over the years and features a single-story porch that extends across the front, with multiple tall chimneys rising above several meandering additions. The Lloyds raised four children in the home, including their son William Bross Lloyd, a founder of the Communist Labor Party. Dubbed "the millionaire red," William Lloyd was one of twenty found guilty in 1920 of conspiring to overthrow the US government.

Today a bronze statue, dated to 1914 by sculptor Charles Oscar Haag and known locally as the "Everyman" marks the corner of Sheridan and Lloyd Place. Engraved on the "cornerstone of the castle" is another phrase: "NO TENEMENTS FOR SOME AND CASTLES FOR OTHERS."

Frances Willard Residence, 1881
1730 Chicago Avenue, Evanston; (847) 328-7500; franceswillardhouse.org; entrance fee charged

This charming house, with its board and batten siding and long pointed windows, is located in north suburban Evanston and was home to Frances Willard for decades. Willard (1839–1898) was one of the most prominent social reformers of the nineteenth century, and the basis of modern social welfare policies can be found in her initiatives. The plaque in front of her home reminds the casual passerby that many things we commonly take for granted today, including women's marriage, property, and citizenship rights, were influenced by her work.

The Willard family came to Evanston in the late 1850s when the population hovered around 500. Frances was well educated—she graduated from North-Western Female College in 1859. Her father Josiah built this home for the Willard family on a parcel of swampy terrain in 1865. At the time, books published by Andrew Jackson Downing provided the country's growing population with visions of the ideal home.

Willard Residence. Kevin Eatinger

He believed that a house would lend its influence "to an increased refinement and moral elevation" of those who lived in and visited it.

Although best known as the president of the Women's Christian Temperance Union (WCTU), Frances Willard was a leading activist in many important reform movements, including women's suffrage, economic and religious rights, education, labor and prison reform, and she was an advocate for world peace. Under her leadership the WCTU grew to be the largest women's organization in the country, and she increasingly saw its role as an organization for broad social and political change and called this wide program her "Do Everything" policy.

Willard began to suffer from increasingly poor health at a time when she was recognized worldwide for her advocacy. Frances E. Willard died in February 1898 at the age of 58. Her work was important long after her death, influential in securing the passage of the 18th (Prohibition, 1919) and 19th (Women's right to vote, 1920) Amendments to the US Constitution. Today the Center for Women's History and Leadership maintains responsibility for the care and management of the property. Reflecting Willard's influence, Evanston remained "dry" until the 1970s.

Henry Gerber Residence, 1924–1925
1710 North Crilly Court, Chicago; a private residence not open to the public

This series of limestone row houses was built by developer Daniel Crilly in 1885, on a secluded one-block street on Chicago's Near North Side. Number 1710 is significant for its association with the founding of the first organization in the country dedicated to advocating for the rights of homosexuals. Located in the city's Old Town neighborhood, this was a boarding house when Henry Gerber (1892–1972) lived here in the mid-1920s.

Having completed his tour of duty in the Army, twenty-three-year-old Gerber left Germany in 1922 to return to his adopted country. During his three years overseas Gerber witnessed a more open homosexual community, which instilled in him a sense that the same could be possible in America.

Gerber took risks that few others were enthusiastic to do, even though gay communities were growing in Chicago as cultural mores loosened during the Roaring Twenties. The National Park Service noted "gay subculture was largely relegated to saloons, speakeasies, and the realm of prostitution," occupying a marginalized place in society that was often viewed as lascivious and treated as criminal.

In December 1924, Gerber and six allies founded America's first known gay rights organization, Society for Human Rights. As the secretary of the organization, he wrote the mission statement and filed for non-profit status. The establishment

Crilly Court. Susan O'Connor

of the Society marked a defining moment in the history of homosexuality in the United States.

Gerber began a newsletter called *Friendship and Freedom* to spread the word about the work of the Society; only two issues were ever printed. Police responded to the publication by raiding his room in this house and seizing all documents related to the Society. Gerber was jailed for three days, and, although no charges were filed against him, negative publicity followed. Gerber lost his job for conduct unbecoming a postal worker.

The Society for Human Rights was disbanded, and Gerber went back to living a low-profile life. He continued to write about the plight of homosexuals, while networking with gay allies. Despite his pioneering work, later LGBTQ activists knew little of Gerber; the police raid effectively expunged him.

It was not until 1963 that a new organization published *One*, a magazine that brought his work to light. And in 2015, the Henry Gerber House became the nation's second National Historic Landmark designated for its association with LGBTQ history.

TO NEW HEIGHTS

ILLINOIS 1888–1916

Make no little plans; they have no magic to stir men's blood and probably themselves will not be realized. Make big plans; aim high in hope and work.

—Attributed to Daniel Burnham

Monadnock Building, south façade, Holabird & Roche. Kevin Eatinger

The Rookery, 1888
209 South LaSalle Street, Chicago; (312) 553-6100;
therookerybuilding.com

The Great Chicago Fire of 1871 has traditionally been thought of as a turning point in the city's history. While devastating, it was a momentary setback, for in the aftermath the city proved its greatness, and an era of even greater expansion began. Chicago's strategic Midwestern location made certain that the city would be rebuilt, and the breadth of devastation provided the opportunity for planning on a massive scale.

Architects flocked to the city to participate in the rebuilding. The potential of Chicago's business district was demonstrated with William Le Baron Jenney's 1884 design of the Home Insurance Building and other innovative buildings—multistory structures that would transform the landscape of America's cities. The new business district heralded the future: buildings were taller due to the introduction of the elevator and inner frames of steel. Within a decade Chicago turned from an old-fashioned walking city into a comparatively modern metropolis.

Amid the atmosphere of experimentation and innovation that defined the post-fire period, the architectural firm of Burnham & Root rose to prominence. Daniel H. Burnham (1846–1912) and John Wellborn Root (1850–1891) formed their partnership in 1873. Each partner brought unique talents to the firm. Burnham had solid business judgment and indispensable sales skills, while Root was the creative genius. By the time they received the commission for The Rookery in 1885, the firm

The Rookery. Kevin Eatinger

Rookery interior court, Frank Lloyd Wright. Kevin Eatinger

was responsible for the design of several influential commercial buildings in Chicago, beginning with their ten-story Montauk Building constructed in 1882.

Erected at the corner of LaSalle and Adams Streets in the heart of the financial district, The Rookery was one of the tallest buildings in the world at its completion in 1888. Rising eleven stories, the building was named for temporary structures erected on the site following the fire. The (short-lived) city hall and water tower were commonly referred to as "the rookery" for the gregarious crows that nested in the eaves. Root memorialized this tale by incorporating a pair of carved birds into the Romanesque archway of the main entrance on LaSalle Street.

The building has a transitional structure, incorporating masonry piers supporting the exterior walls with an inner frame of steel and iron, heralding the beginning of a new age in architecture. Additionally the building offered other new amenities: passenger elevators, fireproof construction, and electric lighting. Hollow and square in plan, the heart of the building was a two-story light court of iron and glass, conceived to deliver as much light as possible to the interior to enhance the novel electric lighting.

In 1905 Frank Lloyd Wright received the commission to modernize the interior court. The luminous and brilliantly articulated inner courtyard retained the grandeur of Root's plan, reimagined with a spiraling cast-iron staircase, ornamental metalwork that honored the exterior adornment, and gold leaf–incised Carrara marble. The Frank Lloyd Wright Trust said the renovation resulted "in one of the most luxurious interiors" of the architect's career.

A foundation of Chicago's rich architectural history, The Rookery was meticulously restored to its 1905 appearance in 1992.

The Auditorium, 1889
50 East Ida B. Wells Drive, Chicago; (312) 341-2300; auditoriumtheater.org

On December 11, 1889, the curtain rose for the first time in the theater of the Auditorium Building. The cream of Chicago society, men in white ties and women in long flowing dresses, arrived in horse-drawn carriages for the first performance of the Grand Italian Opera's production of Romeo and Juliet. At this major social event of the season, the theater was dedicated by President Benjamin Harrison.

The young architectural firm of Adler & Sullivan designed the building, pushing the limits of modern architecture to create Chicago's first multi-use building—housing offices, shops, hotel facilities, and dining rooms in addition to the 3,901-seat theater.

The concept for the Auditorium Theatre began with Chicago businessman Ferdinand Wythe Peck (1848–1924). Born in Chicago to one of the city's wealthiest and most influential families, Peck made his fortune in real estate. He was a strong supporter of artistic and cultural events; he founded the Chicago Auditorium Association

The Auditorium. William Zbaren

in December 1886. He envisioned the world's largest, grandest, and most expensive theater, and endeavored to create a venue that would bring art to all the people of Chicago. Peck entrusted the young firm of Adler & Sullivan with the Auditorium Building project.

Like other partnerships of the time, the architects' talents complemented each other: David Adler (1882–1949) was recognized as an outstanding acoustical and structural engineer, while Louis Sullivan (1856–1924) was famous for his design and ornament. Over the course of fifteen years Adler & Sullivan designed approximately 180 buildings; the Auditorium is considered to be their finest achievement.

Adler's later buildings would rise on a foundation of caissons; this large, heavy structure was one of the last built in the city to rest on sand and mud. The theater's acoustics, ventilation, electric lighting and hydraulic lift systems also were tributes to his engineering genius.

For all Adler's structural innovations, it was the design of the building that evoked awe. Sullivan emphasized the form of a building with a bold use of ornaments, incorporating them into an organic whole. The sweeping stairways, carved columns, magnificent arches, stenciled wall patterns, radiant murals and art glass epitomized the opulence of the era.

Although the Auditorium opened to immense critical acclaim, the building was never financially successful for its investors. What began as a masterfully designed opera house gradually fell into disrepair; by the 1920s the Auditorium Association was in bankruptcy. Bids to demolish the building were taken in the 1930s, but the

Interior, The Auditorium. William Zbaren

cost of demolition for the sturdy structure was said to be greater than the value of the land. In 1946 the Auditorium was bought by newly formed Roosevelt University as a downtown campus, although they lacked the money for restoration. Two decades later architect Harry Weese oversaw the much-needed work, and the brilliantly restored theater reopened to the public with George Balanchine's *A Midsummer Night's Dream* performed by the New York City Ballet.

South Dearborn Street—Printing House Row Historic District

The late nineteenth century was a time of explosive growth in Chicago. The population grew exponentially in the decades after the Great Chicago Fire. Railroad trains connected Chicago to municipalities across the country, and the city was selected to host the 1893 World's Columbian Exposition. As Chicago began to earn international recognition, savvy real estate investors sensed financial opportunity and invested in numerous speculative commercial buildings in downtown, including the South Dearborn/Printer's Row District at the south end of the "Loop."

After the completion of Dearborn Street Station on Polk Street in 1885, the nearby area began to develop as a center for publishing and printing. Chicago was second only to New York in these fields, and easy access to rail transportation was key. The heart of the Printer's Row District—a two-block area between Ida B. Wells Drive and Polk Street along Dearborn—features numerous examples of buildings designed by a group of architects whose work is known as the "First Chicago School."

Their work would have a profound effect upon architecture and its beginnings can be traced to the office of William Le Baron Jenney. His firm became the training ground for leading architects of the First Chicago School, including, among others, Martin Roche, William Holabird, and Louis Sullivan. Jenney's 1884 Home Insurance Company, designed with an iron (later steel) skeleton to bear the weight of the structure, was highly influential.

While costly, this new method of construction had overwhelming advantages. Thin curtain walls hung from the steel frame permitted a more open and flexible interior. Exterior brick walls were no longer an essential element holding up the building, and their solidity was replaced by large expanses of plate glass—an important consideration in the early era of electric lighting. Thus the "Chicago window" originated: a three-part window with a large, fixed center panel flanked by smaller double-hung sash windows, providing ventilation as well as light.

There are four "Chicago School" buildings designated as National Historic Landmarks: the Manhattan (1891), the Fisher (1896), the Old Colony (1893–94), and the Monadnock (1880–91).

Lakeside Press. Kevin Eatinger

The South Dearborn Street–Printing House Row Historic District overlaps with the neighborhood commonly referred to as Printers' Row. We will take a slight detour south of the four landmarked buildings to consider its impact.

Coinciding with new methods of construction were technological advances in power printing presses. This led to the building of large-scale printing plants—tall, narrow loft-style buildings housing rows of presses in rooms with good natural light.

Buildings of this formula in the Printer's Row neighborhood include the Lakeside Press Building at 731 South Plymouth Court. This was noted architect Howard van Doren Shaw's first commercial building. It was completed in two stages: the southern half was completed in 1897, while the four northern bays were finished in 1901. His design featured cast-iron spandrels on the floors that housed the printing presses, with red brick quoins and limestone ornament.

At 720 South Dearborn is the fourteen-story Franklin Printing Company Building, designed by George C. Nimmons in 1916. German painter Oskar Gross conceived the mural over the main entrance, entitled "The First Impression" (of the Gutenberg Bible), and painted tiles depicting engravers, typesetters, bookbinders, and other artisans involved in the printing process.

In the late 1970s developers began to convert printing centers into loft-style apartments. The last of the printing companies closed in 2018, and today the area is highly desirable residential neighborhood.

Franklin Printing Company Building. Kevin Eatinger

Manhattan Building, 1889–1891
431 South Dearborn Street, Chicago

An 1888 newspaper article that appeared in the *Chicago Inter-Ocean* described the new heights to which buildings were rising. The article was the first to use the word skyscraper: "The 'sky-scrapers' of Chicago outrival anything of their kind in the world."

William Le Baron Jenney (1832–1907) came to Chicago in the late 1860s after serving in the Civil War. His firm achieved great success designing buildings to replace those lost by the devastation of the Great Chicago Fire. This work led to Jenney's greatest impact—his role in the eventual development of the steel-framed skyscraper, represented in concept by the 1879 Leiter Building (demolished) and the 1884 Home Insurance Building (demolished).

Manhattan Building. Kevin Eatinger

In those structures Jenney moved from a traditional method of building using a massive stone foundation and load-bearing walls. He introduced the use of skeleton frame construction to support the weight of exterior walls and to take buildings higher. At the time of its construction, Jenney's colossal structure known as the Manhattan Building rose at least three stories over every other office building in the city. At sixteen stories with a basement of solid masonry and an inner frame of iron, the structure was encased in brick with rhythmic bays displaying terra-cotta ornament.

In the twenty-first century, we are well accustomed to soaring skyscrapers, but, according to the Chicago Architecture Center, in the late 1880s, as architects and engineers were just beginning to experiment with skeleton frame construction, the general public was not so sure about the safety of tall buildings (think wind velocity and fire). Jenney addressed that unease while designing the Manhattan Building, and in the end, he made a design choice to downplay its height by dividing the façade into horizontal sections with setbacks.

Monadnock Building, 1891–1893
53 West Jackson Boulevard, Chicago; (312) 922-1890; monadnockbuilding.com

Within the buildings classified as the work of the "Chicago School" of architects, some historians have called the Monadnock a classic—a triumph of unified design. Although the building functions as one structure, it was built in two phases and each segment has its own aesthetic character and method of construction.

Peter and Shepherd Brooks were wealthy Boston-based real estate developers investing in Chicago since the 1860s. But it was their association with property manager Owen F. Aldis (1853–1925) that changed the scale of their ambition. Aldis arranged for a series of purchases for the Brooks brothers over a four-year period beginning in 1881, including this site at Dearborn and Jackson Streets. The area was slightly remote, but with the Dearborn train depot and the Board of Trade not far away, the team believed the site offered possibilities.

Designed by the firm of Burnham & Root, the northern half of the seventeen-story Monadnock has load-bearing brick walls; the thickness clearly visible at the base was necessary to permit the height. Six feet thick at the corners, the structure was strengthened with a hidden steel framework. Before the building was fully designed, John Root died; it is not clear who the genius was behind the final design.

The northern half of the Monadnock has a substantial, simplified appearance, while the southern portion, designed by Holabird & Roche in 1893, is adorned with traditionally inspired ornament. The dichotomy represents the transition that was happening in architecture at the time. The second team of architects preserved the

Monadnock Building, north façade, Burnham & Root.
Kevin Eatinger

color and profile of the original, but the brick and terra-cotta façade hung on a rigid metal frame that transferred the load to the ground.

In the plan, the narrow lot allowed for a single central corridor, with offices on either side, which connected the two buildings. Staircases were skylit to allow light to penetrate the building. When completed it was the largest office building in Chicago and highly profitable for its owners.

But over time, occupancy lagged, as did the building's condition. In 1979 the structure was purchased by William S. Donnell, who embarked on a thirteen-year restoration project in coordination with noted preservation architect John Vinci. In 1987 the National Trust for Historic Preservation selected the Monadnock as one of the top restoration projects in the country, citing the interior restoration and lobby as "a model for preservation nationwide."

Old Colony Building, 1893–1894
407 South Dearborn Street, Chicago

In 1881, William Holabird (1854–1923) and Martin Roche (1853–1927) joined forces to establish what was to become an enduring and highly influential architectural firm. Pivotal in the development of early skyscrapers, especially the architectural style known as the "Chicago School," they used the expression of structure as ornamentation for their buildings, which eventually led to the creation of modern commercial architecture.

An imposing figure at nearly six and a half feet tall, Holabird oversaw the business aspects of the firm. He was considered scrupulously honest, according to author Robert Bruegmann, earning the firm a reputation for absolute reliability. As the senior member of the firm, and one of the great pioneer builders of Chicago, he held foremost rank among the architects of the country. Holabird was an early innovator of the skeleton frame of building that revolutionized the industry, not only in Chicago and America, but also throughout the world.

Holabird prospered as the front man for the partnership with Roche, traveling across the Midwest and bringing in most of the firm's commissions. Roche was the creative director of the firm, with a very different personality. Shy and retiring, he was a lifelong bachelor who did not seem at home in the business world. At the firm he would have had a hand in the overall structure and configuration of the building, but his realm was the small- and large-scale artistic design of the building.

Holabird & Roche's first commissions were largely residences, small flats, and small commercial buildings, until they received the commission for the Tacoma Building (1889, demolished). They went on to design the southern half of the Monadnock Building (1893), the Marquette Building (1895), the Old Colony Building (1893–94), the Pontiac Building (1891), and the Republic Building (1902, demolished). A feature common to these, and many other buildings, is the characteristic "Chicago window," a large pane of glass flanked by narrow, moveable sash windows. By 1910, Holabird & Roche employed nearly one hundred draftsmen and stood as one of the largest architectural firms in the United States.

Rising seventeen stories, the ornate Old Colony Building is distinguished by turret-like corners with curved, double-hung windows. These enliven the exterior of blue Bedford stone and white Roman brick, while vertical piers enhance the verticality of the building. There are six passenger elevators on the interior, which originally housed five stores and six hundred small offices.

Old Colony Building. Kevin Eatinger

After years in disrepair, in 2015 the building was meticulously restored and converted into student residences as this part of the South Loop began a shift from retail to education-related functions.

Fisher Building, 1895–1896
343 South Dearborn Street

After his partner John Root's untimely death in 1891, Daniel Burnham reorganized the firm as D. H. Burnham & Company. Building on his experience with the vast scale of planning for the 1893 World's Columbian Exposition, Burnham became one of the early participants in the City Beautiful aesthetic. He participated in the development of various city plans that culminated in his 1909 *Plan of Chicago*.

Between the Printer's Row publishing area, the central business district, and the new Dearborn train station lay potential development opportunities. Lucius G. Fisher, president of the Union Bag & Paper Company, commissioned D. H. Burnham & Company to design a modern office building on South Dearborn Street. The *Chicago Tribune* declared the Fisher Building was built to "outshine anything of its kind."

The Chicago City Council had been working toward limiting the height of new construction to twelve stories. However, the permit for the eighteen-story Fisher Building was granted before that rule took effect; when completed in 1896 it was one of the country's tallest buildings.

Its height would be but one part of its glory. Golden-glazed terra-cotta clads the framework of the structure, with virtually no masonry involved. This allowed the building's exterior to be 75 percent glass, an astounding amount for its era and more than its innovative predecessor, Burnham's 1890 Reliance Building.

Although the Fisher Building offered tenants many amenities—six banks of elevators, a Carrara marble lobby, mosaic flooring, and offices finished in mahogany—its most distinctive attribute is the exterior design. The profusion of golden colored ornament created by Charles Atwood sets the building apart. Playing on Lucius Fisher's name, Atwood adorned the structure with aquatic details and mythical sea creatures; crabs, salamanders, and dolphins became door handles, while starfish, frogs and ornamental fish were incised on the vestibule glass. This was Atwood's last project—he died before it was completed.

However, D. H. Burnham & Company returned to add a twenty-story addition to the north side of the building in 1907. Except for the projecting bays, the addition echoed most of the original design features.

The ensuing half century took a toll on many of these older high-rise structures, and some fell to the wrecking ball. In 1957 the Commission on Chicago Historical and Architectural Landmarks was established under a preservation ordinance

Fisher Building. Kevin Eatinger

and gradually designated thirty-nine structures as architectural landmarks. These included such iconic works as the Auditorium Building, Carson, Pirie, Scott & Co., and the Monadnock Building. However, the designation was merely honorary—in 1957 the Commission did not have the authority to prevent owners from demolishing landmark buildings and many architectural treasures were lost.

The Fisher Building was designated a National Historic Landmark in 1976. Like the Old Colony, the Fisher Building is considered a successful example of adaptive reuse; in 2001 the building underwent a major restoration and was converted to residences.

Marquette Building, 1895
140 South Dearborn Street, Chicago

During the building boom of the 1890s, out-of-town investors Peter and Shepherd Brooks sensed financial opportunity and invested heavily in the development of structures at the south end of the Loop. The brothers commissioned Holabird & Roche (architects of the south half of their Monadnock Building) to design a structure and hired the George A. Fuller Company to manage construction of this speculative commercial office building. Their Marquette Building became one of the most profitable speculative skyscrapers of the time.

An ambitious man, Fuller understood that in this city one could experiment, and he had a radical idea: his new company would handle only the construction of a building and would partner with architects from various firms for the design. It was an innovative and successful concept, and before long the company became the leading builder of skyscrapers in Chicago and New York.

The *New York Times* said of the Fuller Company, "No other firm in the world played so large a part in revolutionizing the building trade." Fuller had the foresight

Marquette Building. Kevin Eatinger

to coordinate every aspect of construction by hiring a series of smaller contractors, something today taken for granted and known as "general contracting."

A strategic plan was conceived for a building that was named for Father Jacques Marquette, a seventeenth-century French-Canadian missionary and explorer. William Holabird and Martin Roche placed offices around the perimeter of an E-shaped structure; fresh air and light then was able to flow freely throughout the occupied spaces. On the exterior, their design is as an example of the Chicago School style of architecture. It has a three-part façade that parallels a classical column—a clearly identified base with a vertical shaft of floors above and an ornamented cornice that signifies the capital of the column.

The Marquette Building's entry and lobby are richly ornamented with works of art that celebrate Chicago's early history, inhabitants, and explorers, including mosaic murals by Louis Comfort Tiffany and bronze reliefs by Edward Kemeys, a prominent sculptor of animals best known for the Art Institute's iconic lions.

By the 1950s much of the exterior terra-cotta was removed; the building's future was uncertain, as Chicago razed historic buildings in favor of modernization. A catalyst in the nascent preservation movement was the loss of Louis Sullivan's Stock Exchange Building; pressure was exerted on the city to reconsider demolition of its architectural gems.

In 1975 Banker's Life and Casualty Company, owned by philanthropist and businessman John D. MacArthur, acquired the Marquette Building and it was named a

Lobby, Marquette Building. Kevin Eatinger

National Historic Landmark the following year. After MacArthur's death in 1978, the building became the headquarters for the foundation that bears the MacArthur name. In 2001, the John D. and Catherine T. MacArthur Foundation undertook an extensive restoration of the building, returning the interior and exterior to its original splendor.

Reliance Building, 1890–1895
1 West Washington Street/32 North State, Chicago

The construction of the Reliance Building demonstrates Chicago's well-earned reputation for innovation in the field of architecture. In the late 1880s, real estate investor and elevator entrepreneur William E. Hale commissioned Daniel Burnham and John Wellborn Root to design a building at the corner of Washington and State Streets.

Architect Louis Sullivan once praised Hale as one of two men "who are responsible for the modern office building." In 1869 Hale, working with his brother George, patented the Hale Water Balance Elevator, and Otis Elevator manufactured the invention. Hale's hydraulic elevator ran quickly and more smoothly than the steam elevators in use at the time, making new heights of the skyscraper possible.

East façade, Reliance Building. Kevin Eatinger

In 1890 Hale branched into construction of the tall office building, commissioning Holabird & Root to design the steel-framed Reliance Building. According to the Chicago Architecture Center there was a not-so-small problem: the tenants in the existing building would not give up their leases. Cleverly, the contractors jacked up four floors of the existing building on the site and demolished the basement and first floor. Construction began on the new building's foundation while the existing tenants remained above. Once the leases on the upper floors expired, Daniel Burnham partnered with designer Charles Atwood to complete the fourteen-floor structure. (Root had died suddenly in 1891).

Noted for an almost minimalist exterior—with broad plates of glass and double-hung windows—the white terra-cotta–clad structure foreshadowed modern architecture. The structure's vast expanses of glass, interrupted only by minimal bands of ivory colored terra-cotta, give it an ethereal, weightless appearance.

By the middle of the twentieth century, the Reliance Building was badly deteriorated and threatened with demolition. Thankfully it was saved and magnificently restored in the late 1990s.

Second Leiter Building, 1891–1893
401 South State Street, Chicago

In its earliest days, the broad artery of commerce that we know as State Street was a barely visible mud trail, known by two names (Gurdon) Hubbard's Trail or the Vincennes Trace. It was nothing but a path in the prairie mud, worn by moccasins of Indians and a few fur trappers, which indicated the route between Chicago and Vincennes, Indiana—one of the few other forts in the wilderness of the Northwest Territory.

The pathway was improved between Vincennes and Chicago in the 1830s, which resulted in a route that became known as the "State Road." The name was naturally retained when the unpaved mud road was improved. By the end of the nineteenth century, State Street was a far cry from its humble origins, largely the result of the vision of industrialist Potter Palmer.

Arriving in Chicago in 1852, Palmer acquired property along a mile of the street and gave a portion to the city so that the thoroughfare could be widened; of course, that would improve the value of his holdings. State Street became the commercial heart of Chicago's Loop and the birthplace of the large American department store. A century ago, major retailers lined the street, competing for shoppers with lavish displays and eye-catching architecture.

Grand in its proportions yet simple in design, the Second Leiter Building is the city's oldest surviving department store and is located at the south end of State Street

Second Leiter Building. Kevin Eatinger

in the Loop's retail district. Conceived for Levi Z. Leiter (1834–1904), an early partner of Marshall Field and Potter Palmer in dry goods merchandising, the structure was designed by William Le Baron Jenney (1832–1907). The building's main occupant was Siegel, Cooper & Company, a discount department store.

William Le Baron Jenney was the architect of an earlier eight-story building on State Street known as the First Leiter Building, which was completed in 1879. Two years later Leiter sold his share of the dry goods business to Marshall Field and began to invest ever more heavily in land and buildings.

For his second building, Leiter again turned to Jenney. He wanted a structure large enough to provide for the flexibility to be either a single department store or to contain several smaller-scale retail stores. Jenny did not replicate the first building's exterior iron columns, but used skeletal frame construction, allowing for a flexible interior plan. The façade, which stretches along an entire block of State Street, is composed of nine open large bays with little exterior ornament. From its earliest years, the building was considered an important expression of a new age of architecture.

Siegel, Cooper & Company was established in 1887 and moved into Leiter's new edifice. This retail location was not as opulent as the company's New York store, which opened to great fanfare in 1896, but it remained a successful enterprise for decades. When Siegel Cooper closed about 1930, the building became Sears, Roebuck & Company's flagship store, operating until 1982.

Interior stair detail, Leiter II Building. Historic American Buildings Survey. Robinson, Cervin, photographer. 1933. Library of Congress.

Most of the original interior features have been removed from the building except for an elaborate cast-iron staircase. The department stores clustered along State Street began to close in the 1960s and 1970s, as retailing moved to suburban malls or North Michigan Avenue. As this part of the Loop began a shift from retail to education-related functions, the building was converted to offices and classroom space for Robert Morris University in 1986.

Carson, Pirie, Scott & Company (Schlesinger & Mayer) Store, 1899–1904
1 South State Street, Chicago

The well-known names of Potter Palmer and Marshall Field are typically associated with the development of State Street. However, two German immigrants, Leopold Schlesinger (1842–1914) and David Mayer (1851–1920), left their mark as well.

Schlesinger and Mayer first opened their dry goods store in 1872, moving into W. W Boyington's French-inspired Bowen Building at the southeast corner of State

Schlesinger & Mayer. Kevin Eatinger

and Madison in April 1881. They worked with Dankmar Adler and Louis Sullivan for numerous renovations to that structure. In 1898, the partners decided to replace their original building with a new store designed by Sullivan, who was working on his own by then. His scheme included both a nine- and twelve-story structure; construction began with the nine-story portion on the Madison Street side adjacent to the original building.

On May 19, 1898, the *Chicago Tribune* described the building: "The lower two stories will consist of two-story bay window show rooms, making a display of plate-glass, framed in statuary bronze work, of unique and beautiful design. From this to the top of the cornice the material will be of pure white marble from the Georgia quarries. . . . This material will be treated with a smooth surface, combined with simplicity of line and molding. All the windows will be large and fitted with broad panes of plate-glass set in statuary bronze frames and mahogany sashes."

In 1902 construction on the adjacent twelve-story structure began, and this phase included the building's signature ornate entry on the busy corner of State and Madison Streets. The round bend followed the curve of the original Bowen Building but was now adorned with an exuberant entrance—a richly ornamented, cast-iron base with molded terra-cotta above. Twenty-four elevators were to whisk customers to the upper floors after they were dropped off from their landaus or hansoms at a porte cochere on Madison.

Entry, State and Madison Streets.
Kevin Eatinger

Just as the finishing touches were added to the building, Mayer announced his retirement. The existing building and all its contents were then sold to Henry Selfridge, a key player at Marshall Field & Company, who went on to open his own store in London. Selfridge sold the Chicago store just three months later, again with all its contents, to Carson, Pirie, Scott & Company. Carson's was an established Chicago retailer; they had recently lost their lease on a building rented across the street. Carson's increased the size of the store, but

Sullivan was not invited back to design the addition. Daniel Burnham was brought in, and he designed a building that duplicated many of Sullivan's decorative flourishes. Carson, Pirie, Scott & Company closed its flagship store in 2007.

Now known as the Sullivan Center, the Schlesinger & Mayer store was Sullivan's last large commercial commission and is regarded by some as the culmination of the architect's structural and ornamental art. The buildings are remarkable for the steel-framed structure, which offered expansive, light-filled interiors and a dramatic increase in street level windows for merchandise display. For Sullivan, the luxurious ornament was not merely decoration but served a larger purpose—he believed that incorporating the beauty of nature would humanize the urban landscape.

Marshall Field & Company Store, 1893–1907
111 North State Street, Chicago

When the Marshall Field & Company stores were purchased by the New York based May Company, and rebranded as Macy's in 2006, generations of Chicagoans were deflated. Field's had been a local institution for over a century—a premiere department store that provided memories of lunch at the Walnut Room, extravagant Christmas window displays, and impeccable customer service: "Give the lady what she wants."

In 1856 Marshall Field (1834–1906) left his job at a dry goods store in Pittsfield, Massachusetts, and came to the booming city of Chicago to work as a clerk at the city's largest wholesale dry goods firm, Cooley, Wadsworth & Company. In 1865 he and fellow employee Levi Z. Leiter were presented with the opportunity of a lifetime, to become partners with ailing millionaire Potter Palmer. The Field, Palmer, and Leiter establishment operated successfully for two years, enabling the younger partners to pay Palmer back; he then withdrew his interest.

Field, Leiter & Company leased a six-story marble edifice on the northeast corner of State Street and

Great Clock at State and Washington Streets, designed by Pierce Anderson and Ernest Graham. Kevin Eatinger

Washington Avenue. The store burned to the ground not once, but twice, in 1871 and 1877. Undeterred, the enterprise was rebuilt, and in 1881 Field bought Leiter's shares and renamed the store Marshall Field & Company.

Field's quickly became a dominant force in wholesale trade, and a pioneer in retailing on State Street and beyond. In 1892 a major expansion was underway in anticipation of the World's Columbian Exposition, a fair destined to attract a huge number of visitors to the city. Influential architect Daniel H. Burnham was commissioned to design a nine-story annex. Working in collaboration with Charles Atwood, the new emporium opened in August 1893.

Although retail remained a fraction of the size of the wholesale division, the opulent buildings and luxurious merchandise differentiated Marshall Field & Company from the other wholesale dry goods merchants in town. Field emphasized customer service to gain loyalty; the store implemented a liberal credit policy and gave full refunds for returned items. A Chicago Marker of Distinction on the site of his Prairie Avenue home summarizes his vision—Field's was "a complete shopping world, providing every product and service, including the first department store restaurant."

In 1901 plans for a new massive twelve-story structure were announced. Located just to the north of the existing buildings, this classically detailed granite edifice

Detroit Publishing Co., publisher. State Street and Marshall Field's [between 1907 and 1920]. Library of Congress

was the work of D. H. Burnham & Company. Following the new store's public opening in September 1902, the newspapers noted thousands of patrons arrived at a store that was a city in itself. The interiors were a mass of eye-catching products— from rugs of the Orient to furs from artic regions and plumage of tropical birds. There were reading and writing rooms, tea rooms, post and telegraph offices, and nannies available to care for the children of tired mothers, who could choose to rest in easy chairs.

The last major expansion occurred in 1907, when the last of the older structures were razed. The Marshall Field store was noteworthy for its lavish interiors, including stained glass,

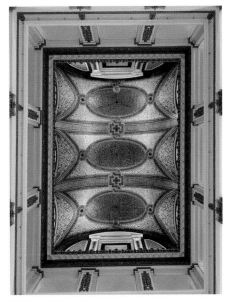

Tiffany Mosaic. Jordan Davis

the stunning Louis Comfort Tiffany mosaic dome, the beloved Walnut Room with its Circassian wood paneling and Austrian chandeliers, and the massive bronze clocks on each State Street corner.

Orchestra Hall, 1904
220 South Michigan Avenue, Chicago; (312) 294-3000; cso.org

Daniel Hudson Burnham (1846–1912) is arguably one of the most important figures in Chicago's urban planning history. As chief director of the World's Columbian Exposition of 1893, Burnham envisioned the "White City" as an assembly of classically inspired structures woven into a lush landscape. His design of the fair has been credited for inspiring the City Beautiful Movement, a philosophy that urban planning should aspire to an aesthetic of grandeur and beautification. Its culmination was *The Plan of Chicago*, published in 1909 after thirty months of work. Burnham's lavishly presented plan reflected a city with classically designed buildings of uniform height, clearly reminiscent of his vision for the fair. Anchored by magnificent parkland on the lakefront, the plan projected order as opposed to the chaos created by the city's rapid growth.

Meanwhile, his architecture firm of D. H. Burnham & Company continued to design impressive individual structures throughout the city and was selected to envision a new home for the renowned Chicago Orchestra, which had performed in the Auditorium Theatre since the fall of 1891 under the direction of Theodore Thomas.

Orchestra Hall. Susan O'Connor

Thomas's traveling ensemble played across the country in the last half of the twentieth century. When approached by a Chicago businessman about the possibility of relocating from New York to Chicago, Thomas's legendary response was, "I would go to Hell if they gave me a permanent orchestra." Hell lost out; less than one year later the first concerts of the Chicago Orchestra, under the direction of Thomas, were given at the Auditorium.

Thomas was never completely satisfied with the Auditorium's performance space; it was too cavernous for an orchestra and filling the venue for individual concerts proved difficult. He fully realized the dream of a permanent home for his orchestra in 1904 when Burnham's Orchestra Hall, with seating for 2,522 patrons and near-perfect acoustics, was completed. Thomas led the dedicatory concert on December 14, but he tragically died of pneumonia a short time later.

The exterior of Burnham's Georgian-style building, of deep pink brick and limestone detailing, has "Theodore Thomas Orchestra Hall" inscribed in limestone detailing on the facade. Overlooking parklands east of its Michigan Avenue location, the interior offers a ballroom for receptions on the second level, while its ninth floor was for years home to the Cliff Dwellers. Members of the notable private club were supportive of or engaged in the arts, and have included well-known architects David Adler, Solon Spencer Beman, and Louis Sullivan—in addition to Burnham.

The Board of Trustees approved a plan to significantly renovate and expand Orchestra Hall in 1993. The project, led by Skidmore, Owings & Merrill, was completed in October 1997. The music complex, now known as Symphony Center, features a new rehearsal and performance space, a multistory rotunda with skylighted atrium, a restaurant, administrative offices, and a beautifully restored and acoustically renovated concert hall. Today renowned Italian conductor Riccardo Muti is the music director of the Chicago Symphony, which is consistently hailed as one of the world's leading orchestras.

THE PRAIRIE SCHOOL ERA

ILLINOIS 1889–1909

We create our buildings and then they create us. Likewise, we construct our circle of friends and our communities and then they construct us.
—FRANK LLOYD WRIGHT

Artist Richard Bock, Wright's friend and collaborator, created these sculptural capitals on the exterior loggia of Wright's Oak Park studio. The bronze elements include the tree of life, a book of knowledge, and an architectural scroll flanked by two storks signifying wisdom and fertility.
Susan O'Connor

James Charnley Residence, 1891–1892
1365 North Astor Street, Chicago; (312) 573-1365; sah.org

Located in Chicago's Gold Coast neighborhood, the residence of James and Helen Charnley was the result of an extraordinary collaboration between Louis Sullivan and Frank Lloyd Wright—major figures in American architecture. The Society of Architectural Historians notes the importance of Charnley House: the architects "rejected historic details common to Victorian architecture in favor of abstract forms that later became the hallmarks of modern architecture."

When wealthy lumber baron James Charnley (1844–1905) decided to build a house, he turned to his friend Louis Sullivan and hired Adler & Sullivan, one of the most influential architectural firms in the country. The partners specialized in large commercial structures: synagogues, factories, apartment buildings, and theaters. This building is one of the few residential commissions by Sullivan that exist today.

This was a time when most architects were trained as apprentices, and Sullivan's work inspired a group of young Chicago architects, including Frank Lloyd Wright. Wright served as Sullivan's lead draftsman on the Charnley project and contributed significantly on the design. The distinct departure from popular historically inspired motifs of the latter 1800s and the incorporation of more abstract forms and ornamentation has been internationally recognized as a turning point in the history of American architecture.

Anchored by a substantial limestone base, with tan-colored Roman brick above, the Charnley House is defined by simply articulated rectilinear forms that give the structure an architecturally intimate domestic scale. The sensitive detailing of rectilinear copper cornices offsets the otherwise unadorned severity of the structure.

The house was named a National Historic Landmark in 1972 and underwent a major renovation by Chicago architect John Vinci, FAIA, during that period. The restoration work followed efforts to convert the modest structure into condominiums. In 1986 the powerhouse architectural firm of Skidmore, Owings & Merrill

Charnley Residence. Kevin Eatinger

Interior, Charnley Residence. James Caulfield

purchased the property and undertook further restoration to the house. It was purchased by Chicago philanthropist Seymour Persky in 1995.

Persky donated the sixteen-room home—with its six wood-burning fireplaces, light-filled court, and abundance of detailed woodwork and arches—to the Society of Architectural Historians for use as its headquarters. The house is now known as the Charnley-Persky House Museum, renamed in recognition of its second benefactor.

Frank Lloyd Wright Home and Studio, 1889 and 1898
951 Chicago Avenue, Oak Park; (312) 994-4000; flwright.org

In contrast to individually commissioned structures, an architect's own home and place of work can often provide insight into the evolution of his or her ideals. Frank Lloyd Wright (1867–1959) used this house at the corner of Forest and Chicago to explore design concepts that would shape his architectural philosophy. It was, in effect, the birthplace of a short-lived architectural revolution. In the adjacent studio, Wright and his associates developed a new form of American architecture—the Prairie Style.

Wright Home and Studio. William Zbaren

A native of Wisconsin, Wright was born to an itinerant preacher–musician father and a domineering mother. Apparently, she decided early on that her son would become an architect and encouraged his interest in the arts. After his parents divorced, Wright dropped out of high school and worked in the office of an engineering professor. He later entered the University of Wisconsin–Madison, taking one semester of geometry and failing to complete a class in French. Undeterred, Wright came to Chicago at the age of nineteen and found a position in the office of Joseph Lyman Silsbee, a friend of his uncle.

In 1888 Wright landed the job he most desired, working as a draftsman in the prominent office of Adler & Sullivan. Wright married in 1890 and, with an advance on his salary, started construction of a residence in west suburban Oak Park. The house began as a modest two-story shingle-covered building. Over the years the house was greatly enlarged and reworked to provide space for Wright's first wife Catherin Tobin, their six children, and his mother.

Wright became the principal draftsman at Adler & Sullivan, working on projects including the Auditorium Theatre and the Charnley House. Although Wright was fired from the firm in 1893 for taking commissions on his own, the six years he spent with Louis Sullivan were highly influential on his work.

Wright retreated to Oak Park where he lived and worked until 1909, using the studio as a laboratory where he experimented with space, form, furnishings, and the decorative arts. He gradually developed his own unique style that mirrored the Midwestern Prairie landscape and redefined the American dwelling. Wright expressed a

Children's Playroom.
Historic American Buildings
Survey, 1933. Library of
Congress

reverence for nature, shown in his use of materials and shapes that could be adapted to specific sites and a variety of uses.

Wright's studio became a training ground for architects and they became the best-known of the Prairie School: Barry Byrne, Walter Burley Griffin, and Marion Mahony. Together they helped Wright bring the Prairie School to maturity, working on such iconic buildings as the 1908 Unity Temple, also in Oak Park, and the 1909 Robie House, located in Hyde Park.

Wright's independent career lasted from 1893 until his death in 1959 and was among the longest and most distinguished of American architects.

Isidore H. Heller Residence, 1896
5132 South Woodlawn Avenue, Chicago; the private residence is not open to the public

After an unpleasant departure from Adler & Sullivan, Wright retreated to Oak Park and began an independent practice. He received several residential commissions, and with each he moved closer to a form of architecture influenced by its physical setting.

Heller Residence. Kevin Eatinger

The house Wright designed for Isidore and Ida Heller rests near the border between the Hyde Park and Kenwood neighborhoods and marks a crucial point in his work. It is one of "the most important surviving examples of his quest for a new style of architecture," according to the National Register of Historic Places Nomination Form. Starkly modern, this residence sat in complete contrast to the traditionally styled residences of the neighborhood.

Heller was in the meatpacking business when he purchased the narrow lot in 1895 and commissioned Wright to design a house the following year. Wright responded with a plan that blended a modern geometric house of buff-colored Roman brick with rich Sullivan-inspired detailing evident at the main entrance. At the third level, groupings of windows are set within columned arcades and enhanced with an elaborate frieze of sculptural figures by Richard Bock, an Oak Park sculptor with whom Wright collaborated on many of his commissions. The interior spaces and decorative detail embrace Wright's new aesthetic, and the Heller House is unique in that it is representative of a transitional period in his work.

Main stair, Heller house, 1965. Historic American Buildings Survey. Richard Nickel, Photographer. Library of Congress

John W. Farson Residence, 1897
217 Home Avenue, Oak Park; (708) 383-2654; pleasanthome.org

Situated in an expansive public park is a striking, formal residence designed by Prairie School architect George Washington Maher (1864–1926). Known as Pleasant Home, this was designed for one of Oak Park's more flamboyant figures, John Farson (1855–1910), described as a gregarious and well-to-do banker, he was famous about town for his attire. He dressed immaculately in ". . . white flannel suits, red cravats and ties," with a top hat resting above, according to the Farson website. Arriving in Chicago with a mere twenty-five dollars, his fortune grew, as did his interests—he enjoyed everything from the first automobiles to gliding on roller skates. After marrying Mamie Ashworth in 1881, they purchased the lot at the corner of Pleasant Street and Home Avenue for twenty thousand dollars, the highest price paid for a residential lot in west suburban Oak Park at the time.

Maher's concept for the Farsons turned away from the traditional Queen Anne and Colonial Revival styles prevalent in the neighborhood. Like other architects of this period, he sought to create an architecture that departed from a reliance on historic forms. After training as a draftsman, Maher worked for Joseph Lyman Silsbee, a large firm where Frank Lloyd Wright was also employed. Maher opened his own practice in 1888, and his work blended traditional American house styles with more progressive European Arts & Crafts–style designs.

Maher's design is highly sophisticated, evident in his use of a broad hipped roof, the balanced, symmetrical façade, and the broad entrance porch. The simplified massing of the Farson House, its smooth surfaces of pale Roman bricks and stone,

Farson Residence. Kevin Eatinger

The Great Hall, Farson Residence. Kevin Eatinger

and the use of organic motifs in decoration and furnishings mark it as an outstanding example of Prairie School architecture.

Maher was concerned with the totality of a structure, looking at the house as a complete work of art. Pleasant Home marks a period when he introduced organic and geometric elements into his design philosophy, which he called "motif rhythm theory." Maher typically used a motif from nature; here American honeysuckle is used consistently throughout the thirty-room house in combination with shields and roaring lions' heads. Viewing the house today is an exceptionally rich experience, as the art glass, mosaics, plasterwork, and carved details have been preserved. Pleasant Home was widely published, and Maher's design was emulated by other architects and builders.

As the house was in the final stages of construction, the Farsons began to acquire neighboring property with the idea of creating an Italian garden. They eventually purchased and razed as many as ten houses in order to expand their grounds. At one time the gardens included a circular fountain, walkways, a playhouse and a south terrace—none of which have survived.

After Farson died suddenly in January 1910, his widow sold the house where they had held many lavish social events the following month. The 4.4 acres, known today as Mills Park for its second owner, Herbert S. Mills, are owned by the Park District of Oak Park and the house is operated by the Pleasant Home Foundation.

Arthur B. Heurtley Residence, 1902
318 Forest Avenue, Oak Park; the private residence is not open to the public

Recognized as an important work in the development of his aesthetic, the Heurtley House is understood to be the first "fully mature" of Frank Lloyd Wright's Prairie Style houses, as assessed by the National Park Service. Comprised of the fundamental characteristics we have come to associate with the style—horizontal massing, low hipped roof with deep eaves, and art glass windows—the house has features that would become primary elements in his greatest works.

The structure is overwhelmingly horizontal, enhanced by two colors of Roman brick laid in alternating bands—as the muscular Romanesque arch interrupts the highly textured facade. However, the most influential feature of the residence is the reorganization of an interior layout typically found in a traditional multistory home.

For the first time, Wright reversed the spaces that would traditionally be found on the main floor with those of the upper floor. The living and dining rooms are on the upper level, raised well above the terrain and reached by a twisting staircase, while the reception hall, bedrooms, and playroom are found on the ground floor. This would become Wright's favored layout.

Wright achieved the feeling of spaciousness in the main living areas through an open floor plan in which rooms were separated by screening devices as opposed to solid walls. Nestling the space under the low-slung roof allowed for a greater ceiling height, while permitting a raised view of the exterior grounds.

Heurtley Residence. James Caulfield

Interior, Heurtley Residence. James Caulfield

Arthur Heurtley (1860–1934) was a successful banker, and a lover of music. He may have met Wright through social connections, as both were members of the Cliff Dwellers, a private club for Chicagoans either professionally engaged in or supportive of the fine and performing arts. After marrying Grace Crampton in 1890, the Heurtley's lived in bucolic River Forest before moving to Oak Park, living here between 1902 and 1920.

Susan Lawrence Dana Residence, 1902–1904
301 East Lawrence Avenue, Springfield; (217) 782-6776; dana-thomas.org

Frank Lloyd Wright's seventy-second commission was the twelve-thousand-square-foot, thirty-five-room home of Susan Lawrence Dana (1862–1946), a forward-thinking, independently wealthy woman living at a time when women were beginning to find their voices in society. Armed with an eccentric personality, she commissioned a residence to be constructed on land bequeathed by her father.

The gift came with a stipulation—their Italianate-style home in Springfield had to remain if any other residence was to be built. Lawrence Dana gave the thirty-five-year-old Wright a substantial budget for the "remodeling," and he responded with the fullest expression of his creative philosophy to that time. And Wright found a solution to deal with the Italianate-style house that was on the site. The new house

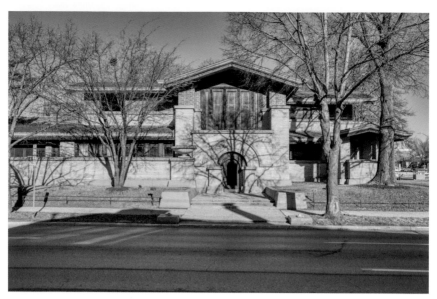

Lawrence-Dana Residence. Kevin Eatinger

was built around the old, demolishing the former as they went, and in the end preserving but a single square room in its pre–Civil War state.

Wright and his colleagues in the Oak Park Studio—Marion Mahoney, Walter Burley Griffin, and sculptor Richard Bock—conceived of an expansive house with a sophisticated decorative scheme. Cruciform in plan, the rooms vary in level and height and flow naturally from one to another. The gallery and dining rooms feature barrel-vaulted ceilings, while over two hundred leaded glass windows and doors are unified by the colors and detailing of sumac (a wild prairie plant), butterflies and ferns.

Wright's commission was not only for a residence but given Lawrence Dana's social standing in Springfield, to provide a suitable space showcasing her many interests. Lawrence Dana traveled the world and entertained lavishly here, using the house to highlight her social and cultural endeavors. A champion for the rights of women; the house became a center for political activism when she hosted social reformer and activist Jane Addams in 1909. Said to be growing weary of her social life, she pursued efforts to pass legislation in Illinois that would give equal rights to women, among other issues.

Sadly, Lawrence Dana's life spiraled downward in the ensuing years as she suffered emotional and financial problems. Ruled incompetent, she was hospitalized in 1942 and her personal effects were auctioned. Fortunately, her taste in furnishings was a bit much for the average buyer, and most remained unsold. Publisher Charles C. Thomas purchased the house in 1944 and acquired the furniture, using a space

Frank Lloyd Wright's Dana Thomas House interior. Carol M. Highsmith, Library of Congress

for his company offices. Two years later Susan Lawrence Dana died at the age of eighty-three.

The State of Illinois purchased the house in 1981 and undertook a three-year restoration program. Today the thirty-five rooms contain an astonishing 95 percent of the original art glass and furniture. Unlike other surviving Wright houses from the early 1900s, the Dana-Thomas House allows the visitor to experience the environment Frank Lloyd Wright sought for his patron.

Ferdinand Frederick Tomek Residence, 1904–1906
150 Nutall Street, Riverside; the private residence is not open to the public

The Frederick and Emily Tomek House, designed by Frank Lloyd Wright and his colleague Barry Byrne, is one of several of the firm's projects located in west suburban Riverside. The bucolic community was planned by Calvert Vaux and Frederick Law Olmsted in 1869; the setting resembles the suburban ideal Wright also envisioned in his conceptual urban plans.

Tomek Residence. Susan O'Connor

Continuing his departure from traditional styles, Wright commented he had a "radically different conception" of what a house should be. The façade of the Tomek residence features a dramatic cantilevered roof, deep overhangs, and strong horizontal lines—in appearance lower and longer than other homes in the neighborhood. In contrast to the horizontal brickwork of Wright's Heurtley House in Oak Park, here the forms are smoothly articulated, using stucco for the outside surface.

The Frank Lloyd Wright Trust explains that the Tomek House is prototypical of Wright's suburban Prairie Style residences; its interior space was much more open than in other styles. The main entrance opens into the ground floor with service and play rooms, and an oak staircase leading to the formal living spaces on the second level. Another flight of stairs provides access to bedrooms on the much smaller third story.

The Tomek residence served as a model for Wright's more famous Frederick C. Robie House in Hyde Park. While the exterior material differs, the development of the Tomek House adds depth to understanding Wright's thinking by demonstrating the path he followed on the way to designing his arguably most famous Prairie home. It is this association that makes the Tomek House an important work in the history of modernism in architecture.

Unity Temple, 1905–1908
875 Lake Street, Oak Park; (312) 994-4000; flwright.org

Situated on a corner setting in west suburban Oak Park, Unity Temple is of major importance in the development of American architecture for two reasons. This is one of the first public buildings in America to feature exposed reinforced concrete, and it is a prime early example of modern church architecture.

Detail, Unity Temple. Susan O'Connor

Interior, Unity Temple. Kevin Eatinger

Frank Lloyd Wright was a member of Oak Park's Universalist Church when it was destroyed by fire in the early summer of 1905. After an extensive search, it was Wright who was chosen to design the present Unity Temple. He responded with a forceful scheme composed of three elements of varying heights: a dominant cubical temple, a lower-height rectangular social hall, and an entrance hall that links the two major volumes.

The exterior of the building is strikingly geometric and Wright's use of unifying decorative elements on the interior demonstrates his theory of organic design. The major source of natural light in the interior of the temple is the skylight, with leaded amber glass ceiling below. The glass is placed in the spaces between the concrete ceiling beams.

Decades of deterioration earned the building a spot on the National Trust's 11 Most Endangered Places in America list in 2009. The budget for restoration was twenty-five million dollars; the building's exterior (originally tan, now gray), plaster, original paint colors, woodwork, and art glass were all painstakingly restored. Honored as a UNESCO World Heritage site, the National Registry of Historic Places Nomination Form likens its dignity to an almost "Egyptian sense of permanence."

Lorado Taft Studio, 1907–1929
South Ingleside and East 60th Streets, Chicago

Hyde Park's Midway Plaisance helped play host to numerous grand exhibitions of the 1893 World's Columbian Exposition. The more formal fairgrounds in Jackson Park were designed as a majestic city reflecting French Neoclassical architecture principals, accompanied by art and sculpture on a massive scale. One of the sculptors who offered significant contributions to the Exposition was Lorado Taft (1860–1936); he received national recognition for the work, and it led to monumental work in the decades to come.

Taft is known as a creator and influencer of American sculpture in the early twentieth century. An Illinois native and graduate of the University of Illinois at Urbana-Champaign, Taft attended L'Ecole des Beaux Arts in Paris. He returned to the United States in 1886, where he had a studio in the Chicago Loop business district and began a career as a teacher at the Art Institute, becoming the head of the Sculpture Department.

The Columbian Exposition greatly affected Taft in that it encouraged his belief that beauty and art should be part of everyday life—not just isolated occurrences but integrated into our surroundings. Taft is also known for encouraging and supporting group collaboration of sculpture and helping advance the status of women sculptors. During the frenetic work for the Exposition, he recruited several of his students from the Art Institute, many of whom were women who received national attention and continued to be pioneers in the world of female sculptors.

In 1906 Taft moved his studio workspace location to an empty brick carriage house along the Midway Plaisance, where the mile-long stretch of Exposition pavilions had been dismantled years before and was once again open parkland. Due to a university expansion in 1929, the studio was moved one block west to its current

Midway Studios. Kevin Eatinger

location, which afforded Taft new spaces designed with the help of the progressive architectural firm of Pond & Pond. The large central court and high-gabled ceilings of the reestablished Midway Studios made it possible for artists to work on commissions of monumental proportion, which were uncommon for Chicago studio spaces at the time. The additions also provided residential housing for other artists and several smaller studio spaces—together these formed a unique artistic community where artists could stimulate and encourage each other in their work.

In these studios Taft worked on two of the large-scale works for which he is best known. The Fountain of the Great Lakes can be found in the South Garden at the Art Institute of Chicago. It depicts five nymphs in bronze representing each of the Great Lakes positioned in the same configuration geographically as the lakes themselves. His most impressive work is the Fountain of Time, located a short walk from the studios at the west end of the Midway. It presents an allegorical sculpture of a hooded Father Time viewing over one hundred figures passing by in varying stages of life, including an image of Taft himself.

Taft was in this studio mainly from 1906–1929, although he continued to work on projects here until his death. While for most of his career he lived with his wife and family in small apartments in the Hyde Park neighborhood, he was known to reside here briefly toward the very end of his life.

Avery Coonley Residence, 1908–1912
281 Bloomingbank Road, Riverside; the private residence is not open to the public

In the Spring of 1907, a Chicago Architectural Club exhibition at the venerable Art Institute of Chicago showcased the work of Frank Lloyd Wright. After seeing the dynamic presentation of drawings, models, art glass and furniture, Queene Coonley (1874-1958) convinced her husband that Wright was the architect for them.

Avery Coonley (1870-1920) and Queene Ferry were born to wealthy families in different parts of the country; it is possible they first met at the families' summer homes in upstate New York. They married in 1901 and led more than a comfortable life, with interests in the arts, the progressive education movement, and the practice of Christian Science.

Frank Lloyd Wright designed a sprawling, elaborate estate in west suburban Riverside for the couple. He considered this low multi-winged complex with broad eaves, impressive chimneys, and careful integration into the site, to be one of his best early buildings. Situated on a corner lot across from the Des Plaines River, the complex originally included not only the main house, but also a gardener's cottage, a

Coonley Residence. Historic American Buildings Survey, 1933. Library of Congress.

garage and stables, and extensive gardens designed by Jens Jensen. In 1912, Queene commissioned Wright to design a school building on the property. Known as the Coonley Playhouse, the structure functioned as a kindergarten for her daughter and other children in the neighborhood.

The project also marked the first time Wright used "zoned planning," an approach that involved dividing spaces based on their function—a technique he would use for the rest of his career. In the main house, the dining and living rooms are raised to the second floor, while the bedrooms and guest rooms, kitchen and servants' area are each given their own wing.

The multicolored patterns on the exterior are early examples of designs that Wright would later use in his "textile block" houses of the 1920s. For the interior, highly regarded designer George Mann Niedecken collaborated with Wright, developing a comprehensive plan for interior ornament, including furniture, art glass, frescoed murals, lighting fixtures, and even rugs to provide a sense of continuity.

The estate was divided into five properties in the 1950s, with the main structure recently restored to its original splendor.

Frederick C. Robie Residence, 1909
5757 South Woodlawn Avenue, Chicago; (312) 994-4000; flwright.org

Nestled on a corner lot adjacent to the University of Chicago campus is a pivotal work of twentieth-century architecture. Frank Lloyd Wright was the most famous of the Prairie School architects, and his work reached its pinnacle with the house he designed for Frederick and Lora Robie. The movement that began before the turn of the century, seeking a fresh and original architectural expression, resulted in a structure that Wright would later declare as his finest.

Only thirty years old at the time the house was built, Frederick Robie (1879-1962) was an executive of his father's company, Excelsior Supply, a firm that manufactured bicycles. Robie's own ideas reflected Wright's philosophy: he desired rooms that flowed uninterrupted from one to the next, an abundance of daylight, and views of the surrounding open land, without compromising privacy. The strong horizontal lines of the structure, the graceful roofline, the dramatic cantilevered overhangs, and the open floor plan are elements that sharply challenged the verticality and boxlike organization of period styles. The Robie House synthesizes all the major innovations of Wright's previous work; it is the definitive expression of his Prairie Style, as well as a precursor of modernism. With low, ground-hugging proportions, strong horizontal lines, and open interiors, Frank Lloyd Wright's building came to define the new aesthetic.

Robie House, detail, south elevation. Kevin Eatinger

The backbone of the nine-thousand-square-foot house was formed of steel beams over a hundred feet long. Instead of using steel as an armature within the structure, Wright used the material to create striking cantilevers. For the interior, Wright's use of art-glass windows and doors were intended to blur the line between exterior and interior spaces. Wright included built-in cabinets and Prairie Style furnishings for the family and once stated, "It is quite impossible to consider the building one thing and its furnishings another, its setting and environment still another."

Wright's innovative design was completed just as the affordable automobile was introduced to the public. Although most famous for its large horizontal eaves, the residence was the first in this neighborhood to feature an attached garage, despite fears of housing gas and oil in proximity to the living quarters. The original design featured a turntable for the car, as automobiles of the time had only a forward, not reverse, gear. However, the greatest effect of the garage was on the traditional organization of the single-family house. The logical progression of entering through the front door, proceeding through the hallway flanked by the parlors, with the kitchen at the rear, was completely reorganized. Over time the automobile and garage made certain that the side door would become of equal importance to the ceremonial front entry, if not greater.

Wright was not present to supervise the construction of the Robie House; he left his family and departed for Europe with Mamah Cheney, the wife of a client, where they remained for several years. The scandal played out in public until her

Art glass, Robie House. James Caulfield

gruesome death at the hands of a deranged employee on the grounds of Taliesin, the Wisconsin residence Wright constructed for them after their return from Berlin.

As to the Robies, Frederick's father died while the house was under construction, and the business had to be sold to pay back debts. The financial struggles took their toll on the young family and Lora left the house, and her husband, in 1911. The property was sold the following year.

While highly influential, Wright's Prairie Style was relatively short-lived and never achieved the widespread popularity of period revival styles. As the First World War broke out the American public became more concerned with traditional symbols of affluence, rather than the unique philosophy associated with the Prairie Style. Yet the power of Wright's work was profound, particularly in his flexible approach to the treatment of interior space.

As tastes changed, Frank Lloyd Wright's masterpiece of the Prairie Style was nearly demolished. The house had passed through several owners until 1926, when the Chicago Theological Seminary acquired it for use as a dormitory for married students. In 1941 the seminary announced plans to demolish the house and erect a larger dormitory on the site, but a grassroots letter-writing campaign against the proposal ensued and the house was saved.

Again in 1957 the iconic structure was threatened with demolition, and protecting it proved to be a difficult task. The Hyde Park community's determination and massive support demonstrated the importance of the structure. Poet Carl Sandburg equated the impending demolition to "Nazi book burning" and declared that there was "something sacred" about the structure. It's ninety-year-old architect declared the house to be the finest he had ever designed.

Although the house was saved, the ensuing decades were not kind to the structure. An eleven-million-dollar restoration project was completed in 2019, bringing the house back to its original grandeur. Tours are operated today by the Frank Lloyd Wright Trust.

THE BLACK EXPERIENCE

ILLINOIS 1905–1951

The way to right wrongs is to turn the light of truth upon them.
—Ida B. Wells-Barnett

Located at Dr. Martin Luther King Jr. Drive and 26th Place, artist Alison Saar's bronze figure is a testament to the thousands of African Americans who migrated to Chicago in the early twentieth century. The figure is oriented to the north, symbolizing the traveler's destination in search of greater freedom and opportunity.
Susan O'Connor

Daniel Hale Williams Residence, 1905–1929
445 East 42nd Street, Chicago; the private residence is not open to the public

The Black community of Chicago has a long history in the city, stretching back to the first permanent settler, Jean Baptiste Point du Sable, who resided on the banks of the river until 1800. According to the Encyclopedia of Chicago, enslaved men and women and freedmen later established the city's first Black community in the 1840s, with the population approaching one thousand by 1860.

The Black community continued to grow slowly yet steadily to approximately fifteen thousand in 1890. Mostly living in enclaves on the Near South Side, the newcomers were a mix—from domestic workers and manual laborers, to a small but growing segment of middle- and upper-class business professionals. Regardless of class, Blacks experienced segregation in housing and public venues, including schools, hotels, restaurants, and health care.

Dr. Daniel Hale Williams (est.1856–1931) arrived in the city in 1883 from the small town of Hollidaysburg, Pennsylvania, to pursue a career in medicine. He earned his degree from Chicago Medical College (now Northwestern University) and was one of only four Black physicians in the city when he opened his practice in what was then an integrated neighborhood on the city's South Side. Dr. Williams's practice grew as he treated both Black and white patients, and he was considered a "thoughtful and skilled surgeon" by his colleagues.

Dr. Williams practiced during an era when racism and discrimination prohibited people of color from being admitted to hospitals and Black doctors were denied employment on hospital staff. To counteract this abuse, Dr. Williams rallied for a new hospital to be open to all races. When Provident Hospital opened in the spring of 1891, a capacity crowd of proud community members watched as the new twelve-bed facility was christened. Located in the heart of the South Side at 29th and Dearborn Streets, the three-story brick building was more than a medical facility—it represented resilience, perseverance and triumph in a time of growing segregation and exclusion.

In 1893 Dr. Williams made headlines across the country when he performed open-heart surgery on an unfortunate man who had been stabbed at a local bar. While the operation was done without X-rays, antibiotics, or any of the tools of modern surgery, the patient survived. Dr. Williams's skill placed him and Provident Hospital at the forefront of Chicago's medical community.

The following year, Dr. Williams moved to Washington, DC. As the chief surgeon of the Freedmen's Hospital, where he continued his work on racial inequity in medicine. Membership in the country's professional medical organizations, including the American Medical Association, was restricted to whites. When denied

Williams Residence. Susan O'Connor

membership despite his credentials, Dr. Williams joined other Black doctors to found the National Medical Association, established in 1895 and still in operation today.

Dr. Williams married while in DC, returning to Chicago in 1898 with his bride, Alice Johnson. After resuming his work at Provident in 1898, he moved to a larger institution, St. Luke's Hospital, and in 1913 became a charter member of the

American College of Surgeons. The Marker of Distinction erected by the city in front of his former home reminds the passerby of Dr. Williams's contributions: "Dr. Dan traveled throughout the nation devising and demonstrating surgical techniques and establishing training programs for interns and nurses. His efforts led to the opening of schools and hospitals in over 30 cities." The Williams family lived in this frame house between 1905 and 1929, as the city's demographics changed around them.

Ida B. Wells-Barnett Residence, 1919–1929
3624 South Martin Luther King Drive, Chicago; the private residence is not open to the public.

In the first few decades of the twentieth century, the city's demographics changed dramatically, as the Great Migration from the Deep South was underway. Many fled to the promise of jobs in the industrialized North, and Chicago was the destination for many Black Southerners. Masses fled the cotton farms—lured by the promise of high wages in packinghouses, mills and railroad yards. The sudden influx had a profound impact on the demographics of the South Side.

Amid a particularly violent year in Chicago, the Wells-Barnett family purchased this home on what had been one of the city's once-elegant boulevards. Tensions were at their height that summer of 1919, a watershed year in the history of race relations in America. Brutal protests erupted in cities and towns across the country. Chicago experienced the most severe of these when the city was devastated by a series of riots following the death of a young Black boy who ventured into the waters of a "white" beach at 31st Street on a hot July afternoon. Five days of intense violence followed, and in the aftermath thirty-eight people lay dead.

Ida Bell Wells-Barnett (1862-1931) was no stranger to bigotry. Although born into slavery, Ida learned the value of education from her parents, James and Lizzie Wells. Mr. Wells helped start Rust College, a historically Black liberal arts college in their hometown of Holly Springs, Mississippi, which his daughter attended.

When yellow fever took her parents in 1878, Ida was left to take care of her brothers and a sister, at the young age of sixteen. She worked as a teacher to provide for her siblings, eventually moving the family to Tennessee from her native Mississippi, where she continued to work as an educator—in a segregated school.

In 1884 an incident occurred in Memphis that prompted Wells-Barnett to begin her lifelong quest for equality. After ignoring a conductor's order to sit in a segregated car, she was thrown off the first-class section of a train. She filed a lawsuit for unfair treatment, as she had had a first-class ticket, but also had brown skin. Although she ultimately lost the case, the effort foreshadowed her lifelong fight for racial justice.

Wells-Barnett turned her attention to white mob violence after the death of one of her friends. In 1892 a pajama-clad Thomas Moss was dragged out of a Memphis

Wells-Barnett Residence. Susan O'Connor

jail by a mob and murdered, reportedly over a game of marbles. Wells-Barnett set out to investigate the incident and other lynching cases, and she published her findings in a series of fiery editorials. She became co-owner of the *Memphis Free Speech and Headlight* that year and Wells-Barnett took on racism with her powerful reporting. Her research concluded whites used lynching "to get rid of Negroes who were acquiring wealth and property . . . and thus keep the race terrorized."

Her reporting enraged local Tennesseans; her offices were destroyed, and the threats became so violent she was forced to move. Wells came to Chicago in 1893, and joined other Black leaders in calling for a boycott of the 1893 World's Columbian Exposition. When the Exposition Committee was accused of ignoring African Americans and negatively portraying their community, fair officials offered a special idea. Wells considered "Colored American Day" a feeble gesture.

In 1895 Wells-Barnett married her close confidant, lawyer, and civil rights activist, Ferdinand L. Barnett. He was the publisher of *The Conservator*, founded in 1878 as the first African American newspaper in Chicago. Theirs was an atypically modern relationship; she kept her name, and he cooked and cared for the children while she traveled to make speeches and organize.

Wells-Barnett founded the Negro Fellowship League for Black men, the first kindergarten for Black children, and, in 1913, the first suffrage club for Black women. Wells-Barnett successfully integrated the US suffrage movement when she refused to walk with the other Black women at the rear of a 1913 Washington parade, instead joining the ranks of her white Illinois "peers." Two years later Wells-Barnett's efforts helped to elect Chicago's first African American alderman, Oscar Stanton De Priest.

Wells-Barnett and her husband bought this late nineteenth-century Romanesque Revival–style stone residence from Richard Berry Harrison, a Broadway actor. Harrison was the first person of color to purchase a home on King Drive, which was then called Grand Boulevard and had been home to the white elite. After the turn of the century, the days when expensive carriages traversed the boulevard were over, but white homeowners were slow to vacate the once-prominent avenue. Harrison and his family were gone within a year after their fourteen-room mansion was bombed twice; Wells-Barnett stayed the course.

Ida Wells-Barnett died in 1931 when, according to the National Park Service, "the terrors of lynching still raged and before the legacy of her tireless crusade for justice was fully realized." Nearly ninety years later, the Civil Rights advocate was posthumously awarded a Pulitzer Prize in Special Citations and Awards for her "outstanding and courageous reporting on the horrific and vicious violence against African Americans during the era of lynching."

Robert S. Abbott Residence, 1926–1940
4742 South Martin Luther King Drive, Chicago; the private
residence is not open to the public.

At the end of Frederick Douglass's speech on Colored Americans Day at the 1893 World's Columbian Exposition, applause rang out for the leader of the abolitionist movement. Among those listening to the famous orator that August day was the future founder of the *Chicago Defender*. In his early twenties and a student at the

Abbott Residence. Kevin Eatinger

Hampton Institute, Robert Sengstacke Abbott (1870–1940) came to the "White City" to sing with the school's renowned Hampton Quartet.

Although Abbott made influential acquaintances during his time at the fair—including Ida B. Wells, already established as a firebrand spokesperson against lynching and segregation—he returned to Hampton to learn the printer's trade. He graduated and assisted his stepfather on a local newspaper; however, Chicago beckoned. Abbott returned to the city to study at Kent School of Law, hoping to make a name for himself in the face of fierce discrimination. That proved difficult in a white man's world; he quit a fledging law practice after being told he was "too black to win a case." Yet his enthusiasm for Chicago was unabated; he remained here and shifted course, determined to pursue a career as a publisher. The son of enslaved Georgians would see his newspaper grow to have the highest circulation of any Black-owned newspaper in the country.

Abbott began with an initial investment of twenty-five cents and a press run of three hundred copies, as he worked out of a small kitchen in his landlord's apartment. The first issue of the *Chicago Defender* appeared on May 5, 1905. Subsequent issues used sensational headlines and graphic images to capture readers' attention and to convey the horrors of lynching and other atrocities committed against Black Americans.

Pullman porters smuggled copies on their train routes into the Deep South (where it was forbidden); there articles were read aloud in segregated barber shops and Black churches. The *Chicago Defender* soon became the most widely circulated Black newspaper of the time—a leading national voice for Black Americans and an unapologetic advocate for civil rights.

During the First World War, the *Chicago Defender* waged an aggressive campaign in support of "The Great Migration." The paper published blistering editorials, articles, and cartoons extolling the benefits of the North (particularly Chicago) and posted job listings and train schedules to facilitate relocation. Between 1916 and 1918, at least 110,000 people migrated to Chicago, nearly tripling the city's Black population. The *Chicago Defender* not only encouraged people to migrate north for a better life, but to fight for their rights once they got there; its slogan was "American race prejudice must be destroyed."

Far from its beginning as a one-man kitchen-table enterprise, the paper grew to occupy a three-story building with its own printing press. Langston Hughes, Gwendolyn Brooks, and Willard Motley were among the *Chicago Defender's* notable contributors. His paper's success rendered Abbott one of the first self-made millionaires of African American descent. He rode in a chauffeured Rolls-Royce—a vivid example of his taste, wealth, and success.

Abbott purchased this handsome duplex house on Martin Luther King Drive (South Parkway at the time) in 1926. With its coach house, the property was a reminder of the bygone era of sumptuous living on the boulevard. Abbott lived there until his death. In 1940 John Henry Sengstacke, Abbott's nephew and heir, assumed editorial control and continued to champion full equality. The paper ceased its print edition in 2019, after being in circulation for over a century.

Oscar Stanton De Priest Residence 1929–1951
4536–4538 S. Martin Luther King Jr. Drive, Chicago; the apartment building consists of private residences and is not open to the public

Constructed by 1920, this typical Chicago red brick apartment building was home to Oscar Stanton De Priest (1871–1951). Born in Alabama to formerly enslaved parents, De Priest became Chicago's first Black alderman and then the first person of color from a Northern state to sit in Congress.

By the late 1880s De Priest had moved to Chicago, and quickly developed his own contracting business. But he also became engaged in local civic affairs, and in 1904 he was elected Cook County commissioner. As the Black population of Chicago dramatically increased during the Great Migration, De Priest became increasingly active in the Republican Party and in 1914 was elected Chicago's first Black alderman.

De Priest Residence. Kevin Eatinger

During his time in office, De Priest also worked as a real estate broker and was known for blockbusting: moving Black families into previously all-white neighborhoods. Chicago was not yet completely segregated, but by this time African American homeowners and renters were concentrated in a narrow band on the South Side known as the "Black Belt." Those with the means to breach those boundaries were often subject to harassment and intimidation. Bombing of Black properties was rampant on the South Side, as the white population resisted changes in their neighborhoods.

De Priest was elected to Congress to represent the First Congressional District of Illinois in 1928. However, when Congress convened in April 1929, Southerners sought to prevent De Priest from being seated. Segregationists sought to block the swearing in of Illinois members; the House was then sworn in as one entire body. When First Lady Louann Hoover invited De Priest's elegant wife Jessie to the White House to have tea with other congressional spouses, the event became national news. The highly symbolic and carefully orchestrated event marked the first time a Black woman had ever been entertained in the official residence of the president; outrage followed.

Southern newspapers responded with headlines such as "Mrs. Hoover Shocks Washington Society Entertaining Negro Woman." The furor dragged on for months but provided the congressman with a national voice that he used to promote the issues of racial equality. As the first Black congressman elected from the North, De

Priest was the sole advocate introducing antidiscrimination and anti-lynching bills in an institution unwelcoming to his goals and his very presence. However, his work to keep discrimination out of federal jobs programs was signed into law by President Franklin D. Roosevelt in 1933.

De Priest remained the only Black member of Congress for the three terms he served. He lost his seat to Democrat Arthur W. Mitchell, in part due to the movement of African Americans from the Republican to the Democratic Party. De Priest returned briefly as a Chicago alderman from 1943 to 1947, but mainly focused on his real estate business.

After purchasing this building in 1929, De Priest lived on the second floor until his death. Restoration of his apartment complex was made possible by the National Park's African American Civil Rights Grant Program. The De Priest Building was selected as one of several projects nationwide—representing sites related to the African American struggle for equal rights—for funding through this program.

TOWARD THE MODERN WORLD

ILLINOIS 1900–1967

Like anything that is powerful, it has a power for good and evil . . . and in my mind has the kind of interior of a cathedral with sort of a hopefulness for mankind.

—Henry Moore, on Nuclear Energy

Susan O'Connor

Charles G. Dawes Residence, 1901–1951
225 Greenwood Street, Evanston; (847) 475-3410; evanstonhistorycenter.org

Although this massive twenty-five-room residence is reflective of the Gilded Era of American architecture, the house is noted for the time it was the home of Charles Gates Dawes. Dawes (1865–1951) pursued two careers during his lifetime according to his Nobel biography, one in finance and the other in public service. Dawes was at the height of his fame in both endeavors in 1925, when as the vice president of the United States he was awarded the Nobel Peace Prize for his role in reducing tensions between Germany and France after the First World War.

The Dawes's residence in north suburban Evanston sits on an expansive two-acre parcel of land overlooking parklands and Lake Michigan to the east. The property is flanked by historic homes in all other directions, erected in the same era by other wealthy Chicagoans looking for less crowded suburban landscapes.

New York architect Henry Edwards-Ficken designed the house for Northwestern University's treasurer and business manager, Robert Sheppard. The house was built in 1894, but the Sheppards were unable to keep the house after a financial scandal. Ficken's design reflects many features seen in France's Loire Valley chateaux, which had become popular with some US architects in the latter part of the nineteenth century. The façade is defined by two castle-like turrets rising on each of the south corners, one of which had originally been fitted with a two-thousand-gallon cistern used to collect rainwater for bathing.

When Dawes purchased the Chateauesque-style mansion in 1909, he already had been a successful lawyer, co-controlled several gas and electric companies, founded the bank known as the Central Trust Company of Illinois, and had managed to become the youngest US comptroller of the currency under President William McKinley. During his term, the financial requirements for small-town charter bank requests were eased, resulting in a dramatic increase in small local banks across the country.

During World War I, Dawes coordinated streamlining Allied supply lines in Europe, and after the war he chaired the Allied Reparations Committee. In 1924 Dawes was elected to be vice president under President Calvin Coolidge and served for one term. Dawes's dedication to public service continued when he was appointed the ambassador to Great Britain under President Herbert Hoover.

Dawes deeded the twenty-five-room house and its contents to Northwestern University for its use with the hopes that it would eventually become the headquarters of the Evanston Historical Society, which it did in 1957 upon Mrs. Dawes's death. The home serves as a historical house museum reflecting Charles Dawes's life lived here, but it also serves as a local history museum and historical research facility.

Dawes Residence. Kevin Eatinger

A massive oak staircase greets visitors to the home, while along the hand-painted ceiling are wood carvings of four apostles—a reflection of the original owner's request. Other original features include intricate leaded glass, the ornamental plastered ceiling in the grand dining room and, with its Tiffany lamp, Dawes's personal writing desk and ancestral portraits, in addition to rotating exhibits of local interest.

Charles Dawes enjoyed the greater part of forty-two years of his life here, with his wife Caro and children. Many notable guests visited during his many careers, including Franklin D. Roosevelt and the Duke of Windsor. The house was designated a National Historic Landmark in 1976.

Frank R. Lillie Residence, 1904
5801 South Kenwood Avenue, Chicago; the building is not open to the public

When the University of Chicago was officially chartered in the early winter of 1891, it had neither buildings nor faculty. The charge of its young energetic first president was to create a campus on the city's South Side and scour other institutions to recruit highly respected professors.

Frank Rattray Lillie (1870–1947) was an American zoologist and an early pioneer in the study of embryology. He received his doctorate from the young university in 1894 and was recruited to become a faculty member in 1900. Frank and Frances

Lillie Residence. Kevin Eatinger

Lillie selected architects Allen and Irving Pond to design a residence near campus. The brothers began their practice at an auspicious time in the development of the university community and received commissions from their social contacts and the institution. Their work demonstrates a steadiness in combining innovation and tradition that attracted progressive clients.

The Pond brothers were unique; their buildings characterize the English Arts and Crafts movement of architecture and represent the best examples of the style in the city. Their inventive designs are noteworthy for their crafted details and an influence on modernist architecture—they designed with simplicity and an inherent respect for building materials. At first glance the Lillie House seems somewhat disorganized. It is, however, an exceptionally complex building, with subtle features that reflect a high degree of craftsmanship and attention to detail.

Lillie was connected with the University of Chicago for most of his life. A prominent academic, he was appointed chairman of the Department of Zoology and, in 1931, the dean of the Division of Biological Sciences. Lillie also had a longstanding relationship with the Marine Biological Laboratory at the Massachusetts-based Woods Hole Oceanographic Institute, which is where he met his wife, Frances Crane (1869–1958).

Frances was the daughter of Richard Teller Crane, the founder of a huge business empire based on manufactured products such as railroad equipment and plumbing fixtures. Crane's great fortune meant Frances was a very wealthy woman. However, her conversion to Catholicism and her political views embarrassed her father and made Frances the "black sheep" of the family. According to a 1915 *New York Times* article, after Frances was arrested on a charge of interfering with the duty of a police officer during a garment workers' strike, she declared herself a socialist and was willing "to do all in my power to abolish the wrongs practiced against the working people."

The mother of seven children, Frances persevered with her progressive causes, including taking an active role at Hull-House, where she was a longtime contributor. (The Pond brothers may have become acquainted with Lillie through their mutual commitment to Hull-House.) The Lillies were generous philanthropists, particularly toward the University of Chicago. As chairman of the Department of Zoology, Frank was responsible for the couple's donation toward the construction of the Whitman Laboratory of Experimental Biology. In 1938 Frances presented Crane & Company stock valued at ten thousand dollars to be used as the basis of an endowment in support of a cooperative nursery on campus. Their house was bequeathed to the University of Chicago, with a life interest for Frances. The university took over the building in 1957 and since then has used it for a variety of institutional purposes.

Robert A. Millikan Residence, 1908–1921
5605 South Woodlawn Avenue, Chicago; the private residence is not open to the public

Located near the University of Chicago campus in the Hyde Park neighborhood, this striking three-story row house was home to Robert Andrews Millikan (1868–1953), an American experimental physicist and Nobel Laureate. He was a science adviser to President Franklin D. Roosevelt and the first executive head of the California Institute of Technology, the equivalent of Caltech's president today.

In 1896 Millikan, an Illinois native who received the first Ph.D. in physics from Columbia University, came to join the newly established Ryerson Laboratory as the assistant to noted physicist Albert Michelson.

As a scientist, Millikan made numerous momentous discoveries, chiefly in the fields of electricity, optics, and molecular physics. In 1921, persuaded by astronomer George Hale and chemist Arthur Noyes, Millikan moved from Chicago to the newly established California Institute of Technology in Pasadena.

Millikan Residence. Susan O'Connor

At Caltech, his research centered on cosmic rays, a term he invented to describe high-energy particles that strike Earth's atmosphere. In 1923 Millikan was awarded the Nobel Prize in Physics for "his work on the elementary charge of electricity and on the photoelectric effect."

An eminent scientist, Millikan devoted much effort to reconciling his religious and scientific philosophies and wrote and lectured widely on this topic. He remained a prolific author and the leader of Caltech until his retirement in 1945. That institution recalls Millikan is widely known as the author of a series of textbooks that were the mainstay of physics courses taught throughout the country in the first half of the twentieth century.

Robert and Greta Millikan's Chicago house, at the southeast corner of Woodlawn Avenue and 56th Street, is at the center of a sequence of three adjacent houses designed about 1907 by Thomas Talmadge and Vernon Watson. Their firm was closely associated with the work of other Prairie School architects, but they were not as daring in their use of form. Watson is credited with the term "Chicago School" of architecture, writing in *Architectural Review* of the work of his colleagues.

Arthur H. Compton Residence, 1923–1945
5637 South Woodlawn Avenue, Chicago; the private residence is not open to the public

The symmetrical, classically detailed façade of this red brick house in Chicago's Hyde Park neighborhood was constructed in 1905 for banker Lucius Teeter and his wife Clara by the noted firm of Holabird & Roche. However, the house is recognized, for our purposes, for its time as the residence of the distinguished University of Chicago physicist and Nobel Laureate Arthur Holly Compton (1892–1962).

Prior to joining the University of Chicago faculty as professor of physics in 1923, Compton studied the arrangement of electrons and atoms. This led to his 1922 discovery known as the "Compton Effect" which in a quite simplified definition, illustrates the particle concept of electromagnetic radiation. For this breakthrough the thirty-five-year-old was co-awarded the 1927 Nobel Prize in Physics.

Compton taught at the University of Chicago for twenty-two years, and while at the institution he continued to be a prominent figure in physics as his research interests shifted to cosmic rays. He spent a significant portion of his time traveling to lecture at universities across the globe on a range of topics, both scientific and humanitarian, according to the university's website. Additionally, Compton's deeply religious background, and his willingness to speak about his belief that science and religion could coexist peacefully, made him a highly sought-after lecturer.

Compton Residence. Kevin Eatinger

During the Second World War, Compton worked to create the atomic bomb as part of the Manhattan Project. He recounted the stress of this period in *Atomic Quest*. In particular, Compton highlighted the pressure felt when the secretary of war reportedly asked Compton for his personal position on whether the bomb should be used. His wife Betty McCloskey no doubt sustained him during this period; the University of Chicago Library notes that she was the only scientist's wife to have the same security clearances as the scientists themselves.

Compton resigned from the University of Chicago following the war. His house was designated a National Historic Landmark in 1967.

Nuclear Energy Sculpture by Henry Moore, 1967
Ellis Avenue between 56th and 57th Streets, Chicago

On this site on the University of Chicago campus once stood a dilapidated structure, an imitation medieval castle complete with turrets and battlements. It was only a façade, concealing the west stands of a football stadium no longer in use. In her 1954 book, *Atoms in the Family*, Laura Fermi recalled its stucco walls were coated thick with soot, with huge chimney pipes emerging from the windows and reaching above the battlements. A plaque was erected on the outer wall, essentially in Mrs. Fermi's words, "the birth certificate of the atomic era."

ON DECEMBER 2, 1942
MAN ACHIEVED HERE
THE FIRST SELF-SUSTAINING CHAIN REACTION
AND THEREBY INITIALED THE
CONTROLLED RELEASE OF NUCLEAR ENERGY

Her husband, Enrico Fermi (1901–1954) won the 1938 Nobel Prize in Physics while a faculty member at the University of Rome. An expert on uranium fission, Fermi emigrated and continued his research at the University of Chicago on the city's South Side. The atomic age arrived on December 2, 1942, when Fermi and his team working on the Manhattan Project produced the first controlled nuclear chain reaction in their makeshift laboratory, a former squash court concealed under the west stands of Stagg Field.

That same evening, the Fermis held a party in their nearby home, where many of the guests were colleagues. Laura Fermi was puzzled when many offered their congratulations, but she could get no answers as to what the pats on the back were about, for all were sworn to secrecy.

Although the stadium and squash court were razed in 1957, a sculpture was commissioned by the University of Chicago. British artist Henry Moore, an eminent

Nuclear Energy. Susan O'Connor

public sculptor known for his semi-abstract, monumental bronzes, designed and cast the twelve-foot-tall sculpture between 1963 and 1967. Exactly twenty-five years after the first chain reaction, *Nuclear Energy* was unveiled on December 2, 1967, as a memorial to the accomplishments of Fermi and his fellow physicists. According to the university, in Moore's mind it was both a celebration of this incredible human achievement and a warning against the dangers of harnessing such natural, physical power.

Chicago Board of Trade, 1930
141 West Jackson Boulevard, Chicago; 141wjackson.com

The streamlined figure of Ceres, the Roman Goddess of grain, shimmers high above the southern end of LaSalle Street. Located in the heart of the city's financial district, she tops the Chicago Board of Trade (CBOT)—the world's oldest futures and options exchange.

In 1848 a group of Chicago businessmen wanted to bring order to the Midwest's chaotic grain market, where prices fluctuated dramatically. The CBOT was established as a central location for negotiating transactions and offered farmers a way to get a guaranteed price for their goods ahead of time by offering "to arrive" contracts (or futures) for their products.

The Chicago Board of Trade Building originally on this site was designed by architect William W. Boyington in 1882. The defining feature of that ten-story limestone building was a 325-foot tower; it began to lean over time and was taken down in 1894. The entire structure was later determined to be unsound and was demolished in 1929.

John Holabird and John Wellborn Root Jr., both sons of famous Chicago architects, were commissioned to design the new structure. Their regal Art Deco–style building is the focal point of LaSalle Street. Art Deco was at the peak of its popularity during the late 1920s and early 1930s, and its influence could be seen in the sweeping horizontal lines, rounded corners, and metallic materials of everything

Board of Trade, detail. Kevin Eatinger

LaSalle Street. Kevin Eatinger

Crown Hall. Kevin Eatinger

Mies understood the inherent qualities of the materials he used and developed new techniques to create an architecture that was reduced to essentials. He combined aluminum, glass, and steel with traditional marble, granite, travertine, bronze, and brick to give his buildings a sensuous richness for all their apparent austerity. "Less is more" was his credo.

Crown Hall seems to float delicately above the lawn, reachable by wide travertine steps interrupted by a broader platform. This south-facing entrance structure has a visual lightness, welcoming a visitor seamlessly from the ground to the building. The

suspended roof provides a column-free interior eighteen feet in height, an endlessly adaptable workspace for an open, collaborative exchange of ideas.

Mies designed many significant buildings, including the minimalist Farnsworth House in Plano, Illinois, in 1951, and from 1954 to 1958, the Seagram Building on Park Avenue in New York. After twenty years as director of architecture at IIT, Mies resigned the position in 1958 at the age of seventy-two. Throughout his life he maintained a private practice and ranks as one of the most notable and influential architects of the twentieth century.

In 1968, the local highway department condemned a two-acre portion at the western edge of the property adjoining the house for construction of a bridge over the Fox River. Farnsworth sued to stop the project but lost the court case. She was right to contest the work; today the sound of nearby car traffic contrasts with the serenity of the site.

Farnsworth sold the house in 1972 and retired to her stone villa in Italy. Mies's practice became more focused on high-rise buildings. Both were visionaries and both were disappointed. Nonetheless, their relationship produced a highly celebrated midcentury masterpiece, now owned by the National Trust for Historic Preservation. The minimalist interior is now furnished as the architect would have approved: a pair of Tugendhat lounge chairs, three Brno chairs, a Barcelona couch—iconic 1930s designs made of chrome and leather.

The house was designated a National Historic Landmark in 2006, joining 2,540 other sites across the country recognized as places that possess exceptional value in illustrating the heritage of our country.

LOCATION INDEX

ABOUT THE AUTHOR

Susan O'Connor Davis is an independent scholar and the author of *Chicago's Historic Hyde Park* (University of Chicago Press, 2013). She has long been enamored by architecture, interior design, and history. Originally a Chicago regional manager at Knoll International, Davis went on to write on the architecture and urban development of two historic communities on Chicago's South Side. Her work was the recipient of the Jean S. Block Award in recognition of Excellence in Scholarship related to the history of Hyde Park.

Davis's own home, designed by John Vinci, was the recipient of the American Institute of Architects' Distinguished Building Award. Davis also has served on the University of Chicago Women's Board and as a member of the board of the Smart Museum of Art. She currently works with Berkshire Hathaway HomeServices, specializing in historic properties. She lives in Chicago, Illinois.